In Praise of Beautiful Books

British Artists' Book Makers and Fine Presses

Cover illustrations:

Front: large photo - David Howe p52, red book - Gwen Simpson p73 & star book - Susie Leiper p57

Back: Anne Rook p66

Compiled, designed and published by:
BCF Books
Burton Cottage Farm,
East Coker, Yeovil,
Somerset BA22 9LS
E: cm@craftgalleries.co.uk
www.bcfbooks.co.uk
T: 01935 862731

Printed in China through World Print Ltd.

ISBN: 978 0 9548512 00

Contents

Notes :

artistsbooksonline logo
members of artistsbooksonline indicated by this reduced logo

* As I (Ed) am a member of ABCD (an artists' book making group), I have used some of our images to fill the inevitable blank pages, created when attempting (where possible) to keep the book laid out alphabetically.

It is with the reading of books the
same as with looking at pictures;
one must,
without doubt,
without hesitation,
with assurance,
admire what is beautiful.

Vincent van Gogh

Introduction to Beautiful Books

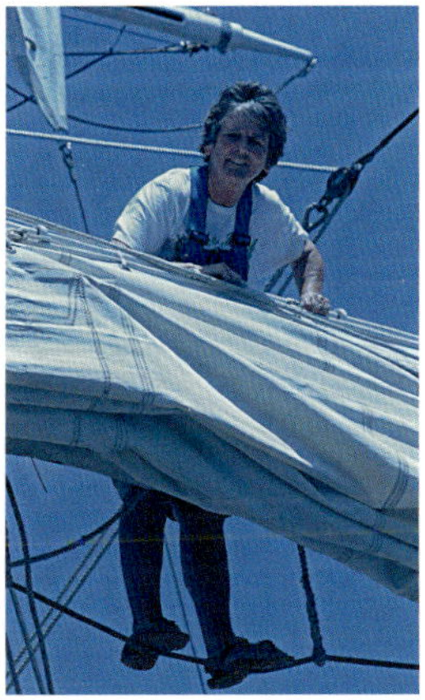

After many years spent deeply involved in the contemporary craft world, I returned to my original interest, a few years ago, when I studied for a contemporary fine art degree. A bonus, during this three year course, was an introduction to the genre Livres d'Artistes. I had found an art which combined my main interests writing, art and books. I felt genuinely excited as I looked deeper into my new discovery - the possibilities ahead were tantalising.

Once I had realised the existence of Artists' Books I searched for books about them and found that nearly all appeared to be published by and about Americans. Many are great books but I felt some attempt should be made to promote British artists to redress the balance.

On searching the internet and visiting Book Fairs I discovered numerous artists' book makers and small fine presses, but of course it wasn't easy to persuade them that they should take part in an unknown publication. I am therefore delighted that over 70 have decided to participate in this first edition praising beautiful British books. By contributing they are helping to share this fascinating art with a wider book loving audience. I am very grateful for their support and enthusiasm for this project.

I realise that for some readers this may be their first introduction to Artists' Books; not an easy subject to explain - they can be so many things. However all will be original, imaginative creations sometimes using materials that may never have been connected with book making before. They can also be traditionally crafted books, printed on an antique press; the possibilities are endless.

I hope that this book will serve as a short introduction for those new to the genre and as a delightful interlude for those already familiar with these beautiful books. Perhaps some of you will even decide to take part in future publications by BCF Books on this subject.

Caroline Mornement

BCF Books published the popular series of Craft Galleries Guides from 1992 - 2012.

Jules Allen

julesallen.arts@btinternet.com
www.julesallen.co.uk

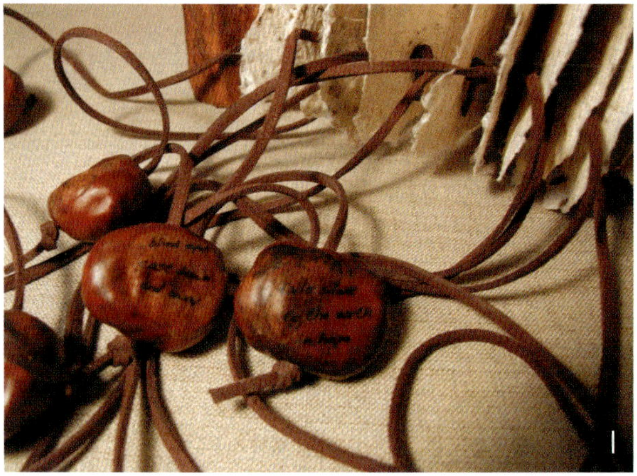

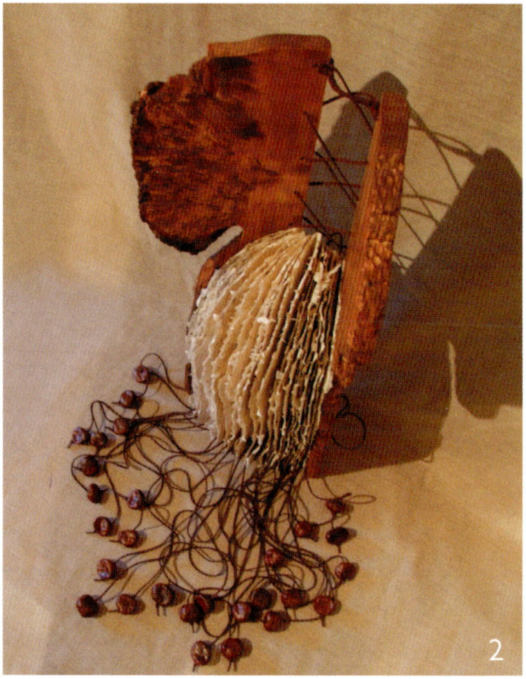

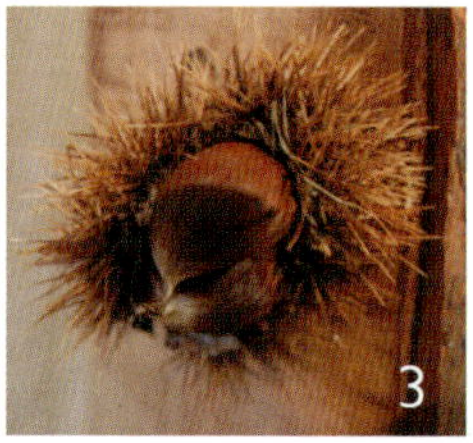

1 & 3

Hope falls silent to the earth (Details)
Poem etched onto seeds of horse chestnut tree

2

Hope falls silent to the earth
40 x 30 x 12 cm
Burr wood, handmade paper from leaves and seeds of horse chestnut with leather bindings

Charlotte Andrew

charlotteandrew@mac.com
www.charlotteandrew.com

Charlotte is a versatile artist, her work encompasses painting, sculpture and text, but the variety and manner of execution challenges the senses. Much of the work is recycled which prompts us to think and reconsider the origins of the material and their ultimate disposal.

This is an original fairy tale written by Charlotte, illustrated by Hedieh J.Ilchi. A suspenseful tale that floats through the pages with flights from hope to despair and back to hope. The heroine metamorphoses into various forms to escape the macabre on a journey to find that "something more".

What an enchanting tale; the illustrations flow superbly with the story and enhance the imaginative forms created by the author. As with traditional fairy tales one is left with a satisfying sense of completion and calm.

Written by curator Madeline Abey-koch

1 & 2
Traveller's Tales
15/21 cm paper and laser print

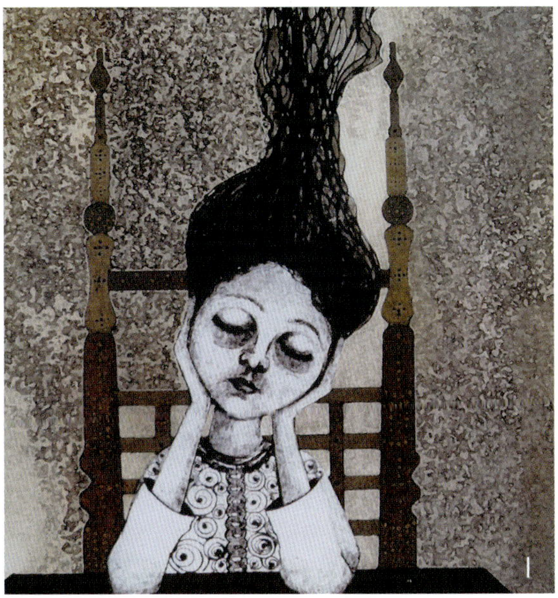

1

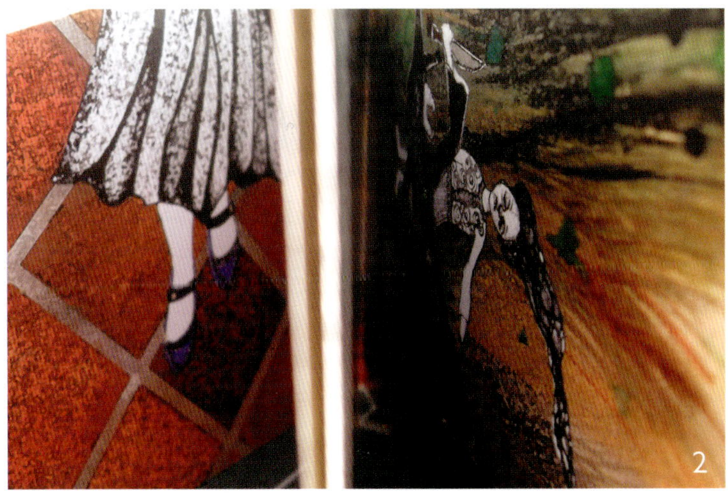

2

Karen Apps

karenapps@btinternet.com
www.karenapps.com

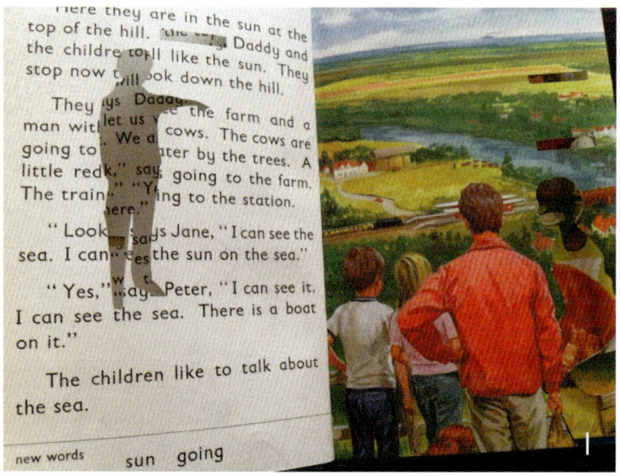

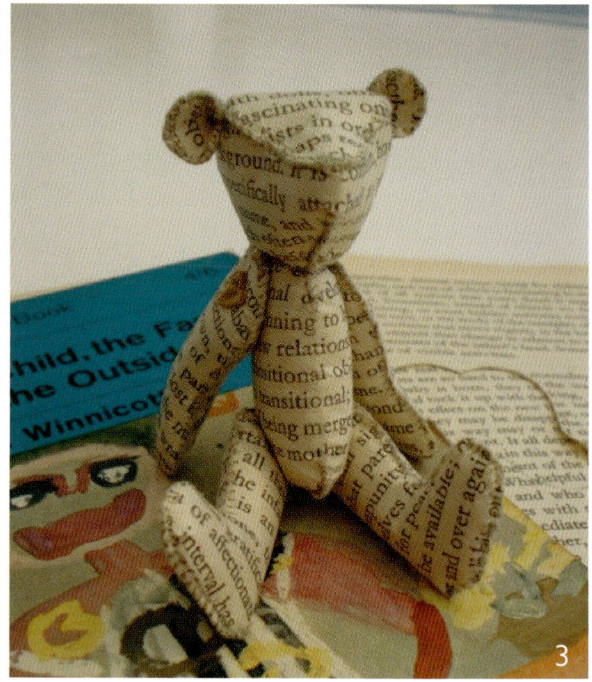

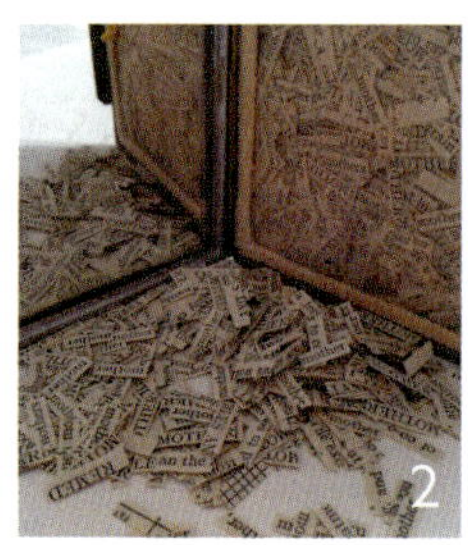

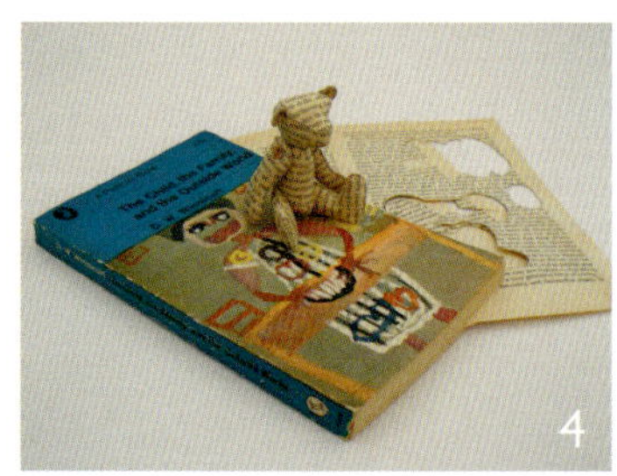

1
Unmothered:
'She learned from the cradle never to cry.'
Altered Ladybird book

2
Unmothered:
'Nothing just vanishes,' she'd read, 'of every - thing that disappears there remain traces.'
Cut text and mirror compact

3 & 4
An object of my own making.
Paper and thread; jointed bear made from the pages of 'The Child, the Family and the Outside World' by D W Winnicott.

ABCD
Artists' Book Club Dove

Dove Studios, Somerset
cm@craftgalleries.co.uk
Also please see pages 33, 37 & 49

ABCD is an artists' book making group who meet monthly at Dove Studios, hosted by Bronwen Bradshaw (p19), to enjoy exchanging ideas; learning new techniques and sharing delicious lunches ! This year we all chose a one word subject to put in a pot, then pulled one out each month - to be the content of our books. Some words were a challenge while others were immediately inspiring and pushed our imagination in all directions. I have included some of our work on the random pages indicated (see blue box).

It is inspiring to see what others are doing and share ideas rather than working in total isolation. Throughout the UK there are probably many similar groups, it would be interesting to hear from some of them for future publications.

Caroline Mornement (BCF Books)

1
What is a Book ?
15 x 19 cm
variant edition of 26
by Ama Bolton

2
Typical 'shared lunch' at Dove Studios.

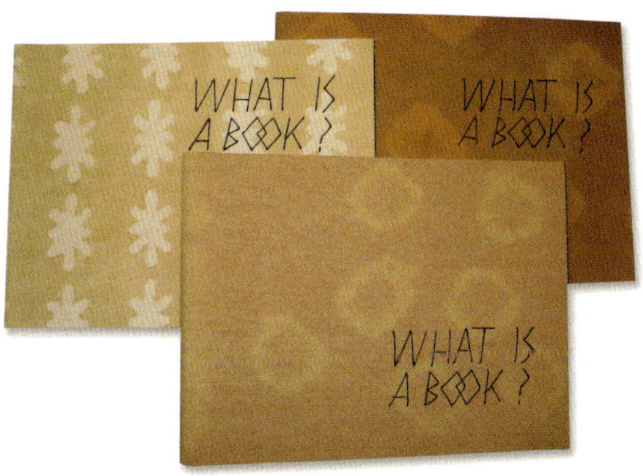

1

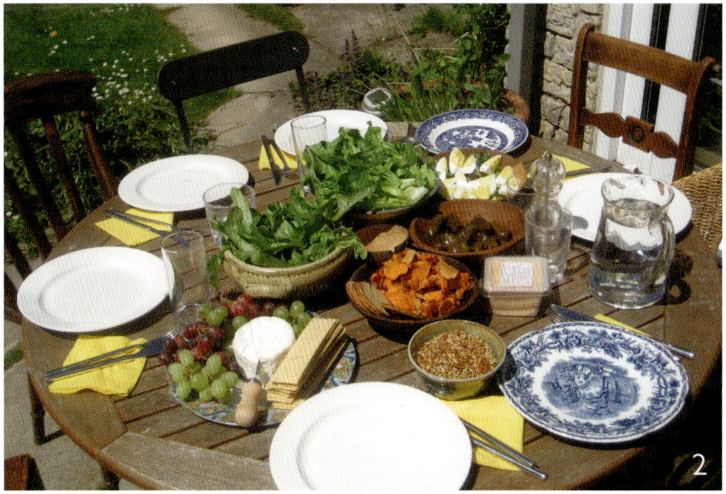

2

www.artistsbooksonline.com

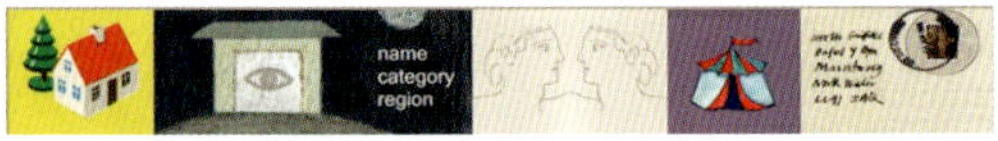

hafod.art@virgin.net
www.artistsbooksonline.com

Artistsbooksonline.com is an artist-run website which brings together a diverse range of artists who make one-off or small limited editions (less than 50 copies) of books. The site aims to introduce the viewer to books made with love, care and humour. Contact details for each artist, sales information and website links are provided.

Noëlle Griffiths started artistsbooksonline.com in 2005. At present there are 40 site artists from the UK and overseas. The site provides an opportunity for artists to show their books on-line to a wider audience, share costs to take books to artists' book fairs, to collaborate making books, run workshops and curate exhibitions.

1

Fig Harvest (2011)
17 x 24 cm closed & 142 cm open. Concertina book, photographs digitally printed using archival ink on 175gsm Somerset book paper, edition 30 copies

2

A Garden with its Birds (2010)
23 x 24 cm
Bound book, collograph prints and digital text on 280gsm BFK Rives paper, edition 10 copies.

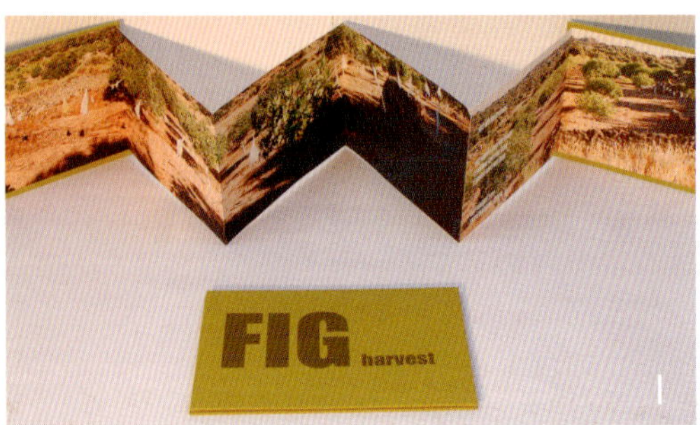

1 & 2 Noëlle Griffiths, Hafod Press

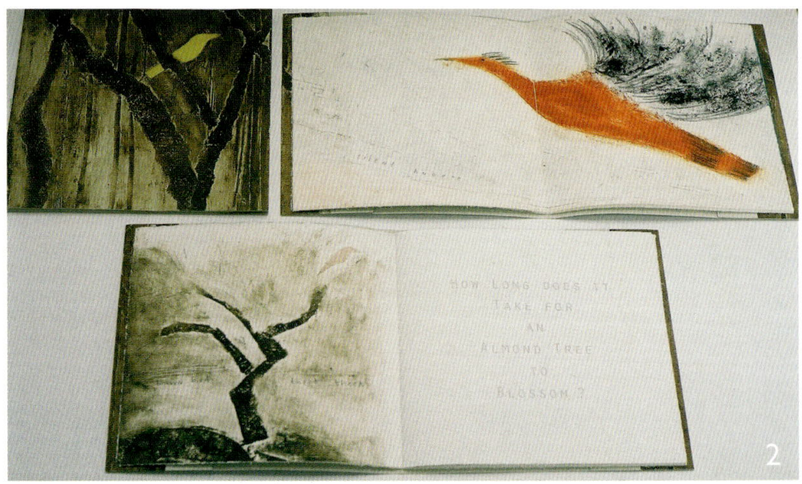

3
Sampling Sunderland Glass
21 x 15 cm Bound book, ink jet print on acid free cartridge paper. Edition 5 copies.

4
kaum/hardly/amper
14 x 21 cm
Cloth bound, ink jet photographs, letter - press text, edition 10 copies. 2008

5
Cocoon Collection
8 x 6 cm closed, 8 x15 cm x1.5 m open. Ink jet print on silk, cocoons, silk paper, mulberry bark & wood.

6
Motherhood
9 x 7 cm Handmade felt incorporating found textiles, hand stitch & heat transfer text and images.

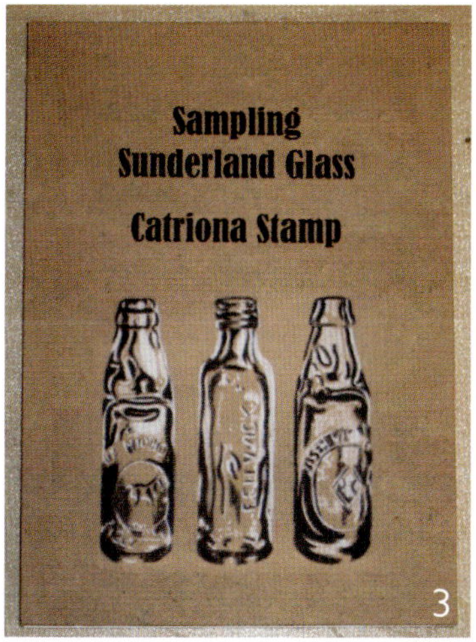

3

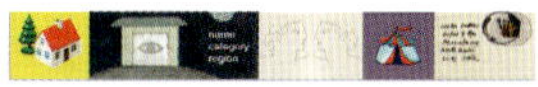

3 Catriona Stamp
4 Frans Baake
5 Jan Fairbairn-Edwards
6 Omi Pharncote

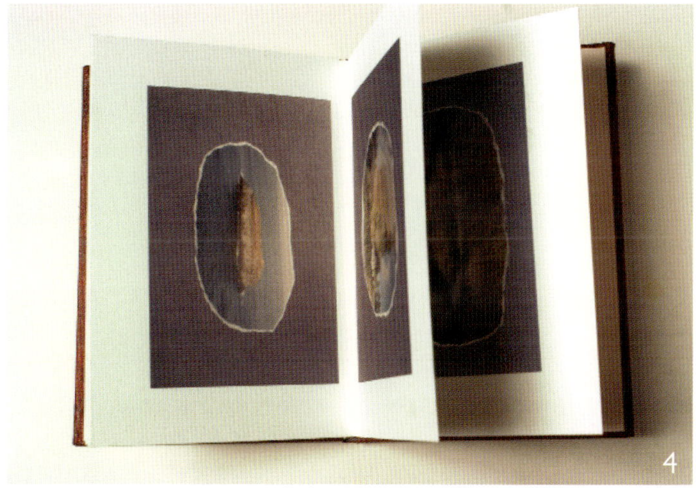
4

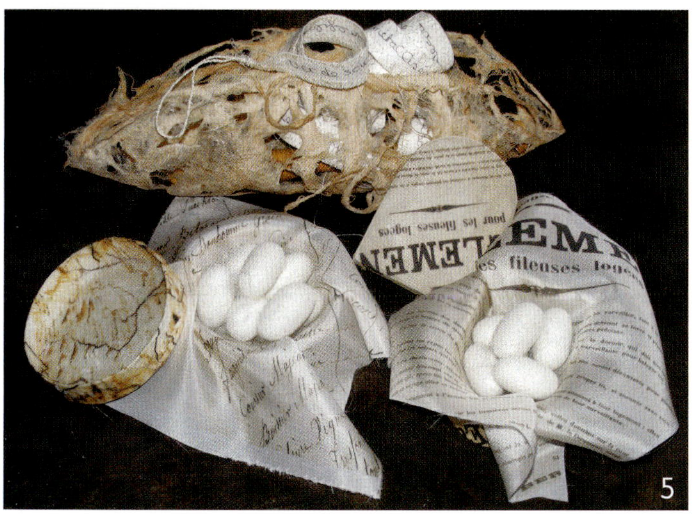
5

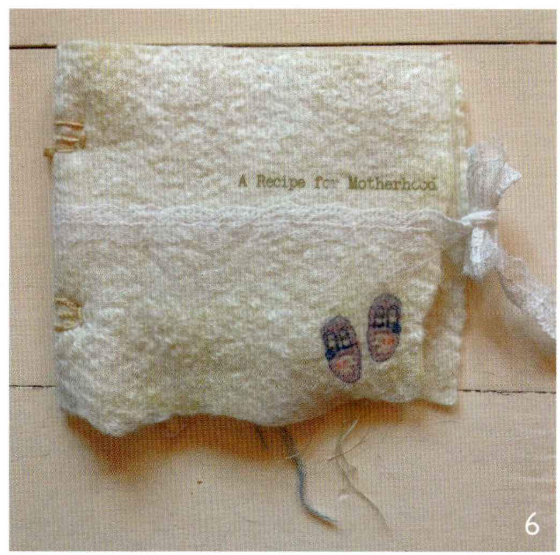

6

Atlantic Press

info@atlanticpressbooks.com
atlanticpressbooks.com

At Atlantic Press, we create works of graphic literature which respect the illustrator's personal voice: their ideas, their pictures and their words. We call this 'authorial illustration'.

Our rare and collectable books present imaginative ideas or tell intriguing stories, and are often illustrated for an adult audience, or designed to appeal to an audience of all ages. We seek to promote new authorial illustration talent, as well as recognising existing practitioners in the illustration field. Working closely with talented illustrators, we allow them authorial freedom; our role is to support their personal imaginative vision. We want illustrators to be enterprising, and most importantly, we want to contribute to a cultural shift whereby intelligent illustrated books become popular with the general book-buying public.

Atlantic Press is an independent press, associated with the Masters course in authorial illustration at Falmouth University.

1
Fried Eggs in Brine by Paul Slater
30.5 x 22.5 x 1.6 cm
Hard back, sewn in sections, with slip-cover

2
The Garden Sketchbook by A-K Laine and Emma Wills
14.7 x 10.4 x 0.5 cm
Printed on recycled paper, sewn in sections, with a card cover and rounded corners

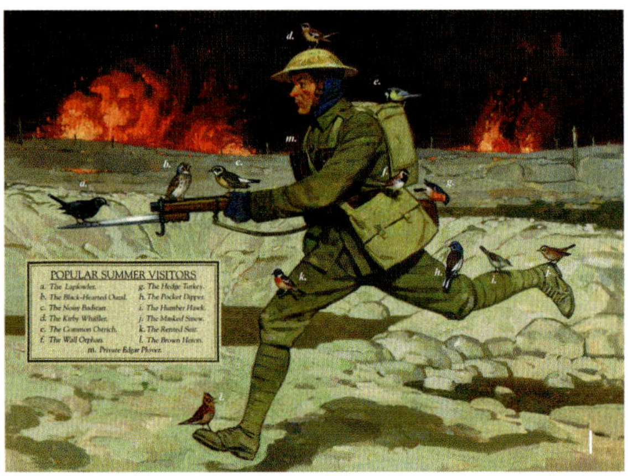

1

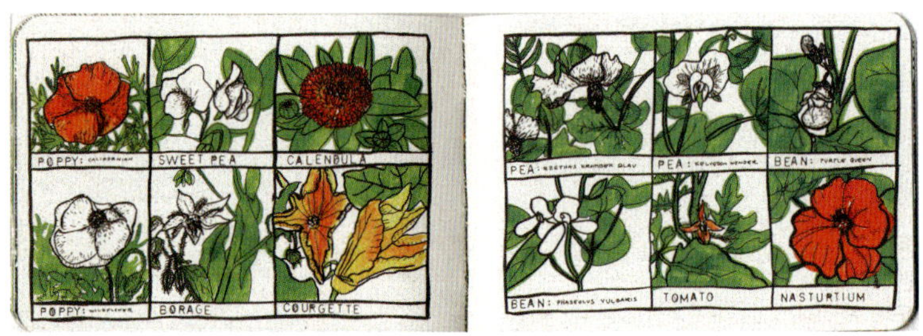

2

3
A Postcard from the Mountains with the Mountains Tipp-Exed Out by Richard Dinnis
19.7 x 12.9 x 0.6 cm Sewn in sections with a card cover

4
The Case by Helene Pertl
23 x 16.4 x 0.4 cm Sewn in sections with a card cover

5
A Book Made of Tears by Dean Owens
14.1 x 10.4 x 0.9 cm Hardback, sewn in sections

6 & 7
Beyond the Wire by Alys Jones
24.2 x 17.1 x 0.5 cm Hand cut pages, saddle stitched, with card cover

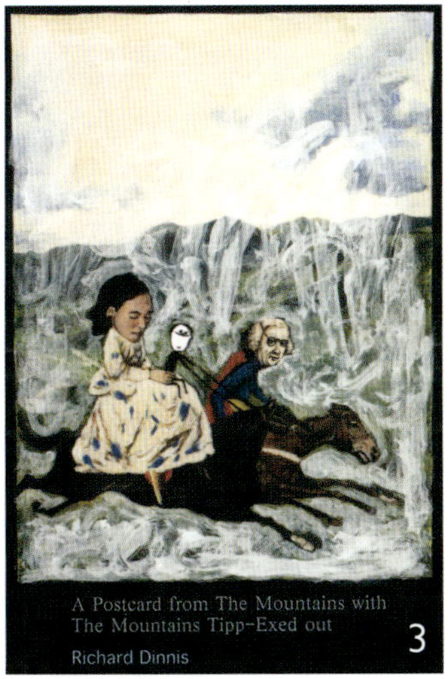

3

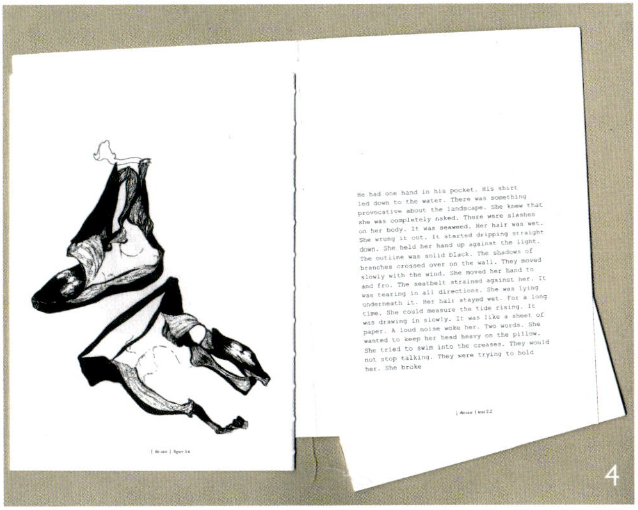

4

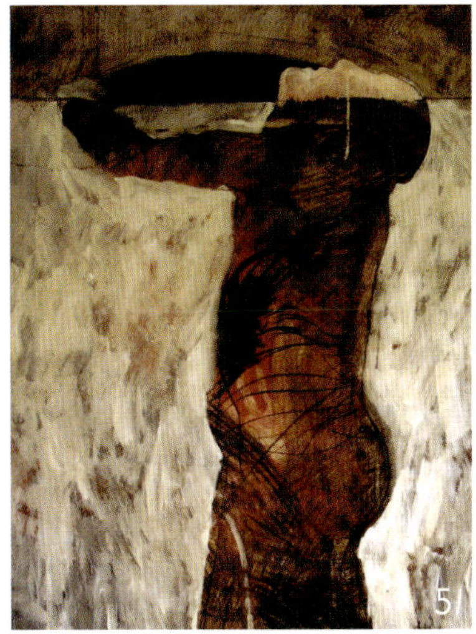
5

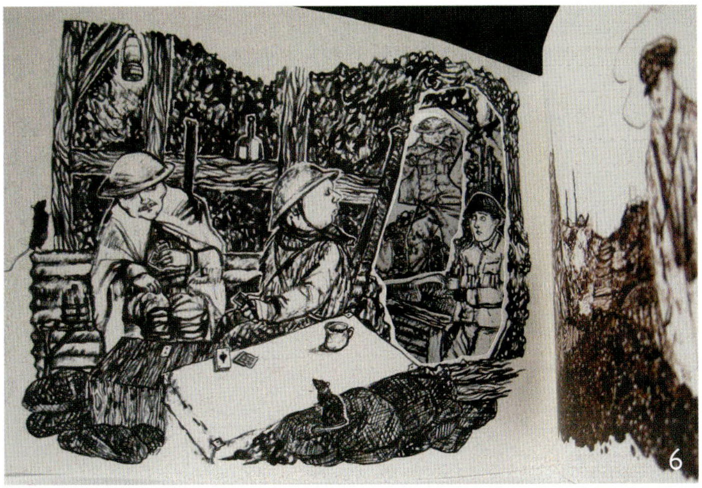
6

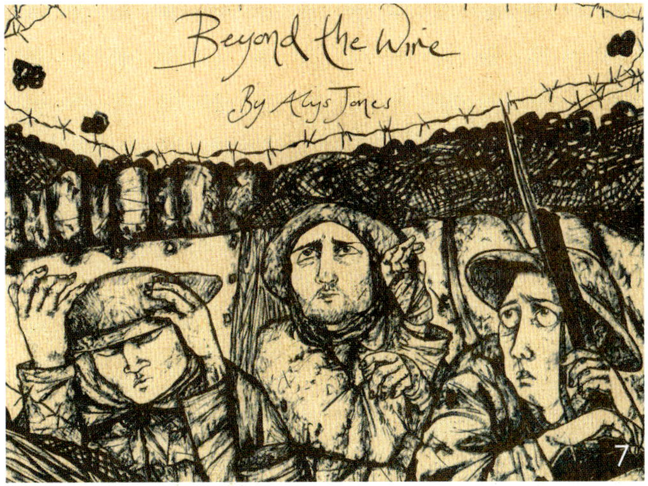

7

Mavina Baker

mavina@mavinabaker.com
www.mavinabaker.blogspot.co.uk

Specialising in relief print techniques and letterpress Mavina creates one-off's and small limited edition hand-made books, prints and posters (max 50 copies). Mavina established the Teacup press in 2010.

She publishes her own artist editions and works in collaboration with other poets and artists and has organised exhibitions of artists' books and print.

Her work is exhibited internationally and is in various private and public collections in the UK, the United States, Denmark and Taiwan.

1

Tales My Mother Told Me
15 x 15 cm
Card, Saunders Waterford paper, hand drawn, letterpress, star fold.

2

21st
20 x 20 cm
Card, Saunders Waterford paper, lino - print, digital print, letter - press, concertina folded.

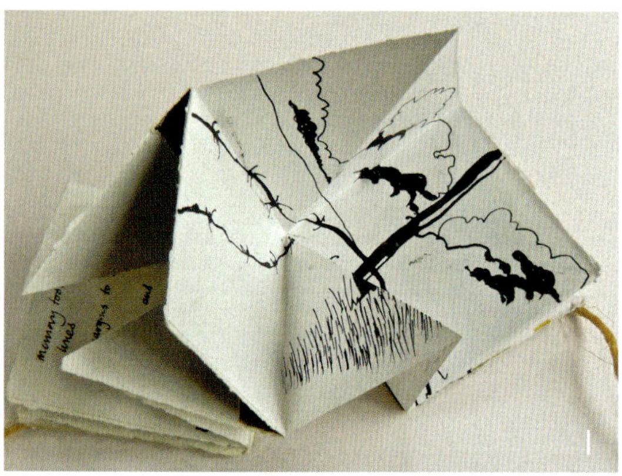

1

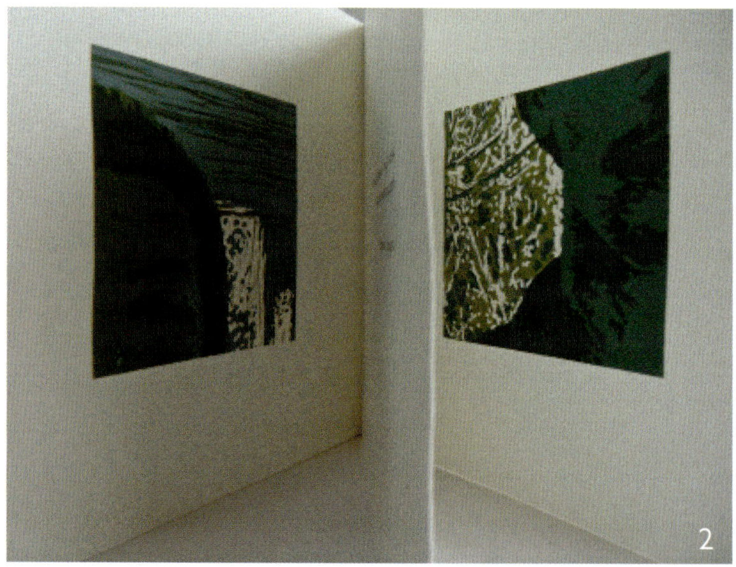

2

3
Old Operating Theatre
20 x 20 cm Cloth bound, Saunders Waterford paper, linoprint, digital print, concertina folded.

4
Fowl Play
20 x 40 cm Card, Saunders Waterford paper, linoprint, digital print, concertina folded.

5
Bella's French Love Affair
18 x 17 cm Card, Waterford paper, digital print, rubber stamp, concertina folded.

6
Falling Gently
15 x 22 cm Cloth bound, Saunders Waterford paper, linoprint, digital print, letter-press, concertina folded.

7
Hidden landscapes
12 x 22 cm Handmade paper, letterpress, hand drawn, concertina fold.

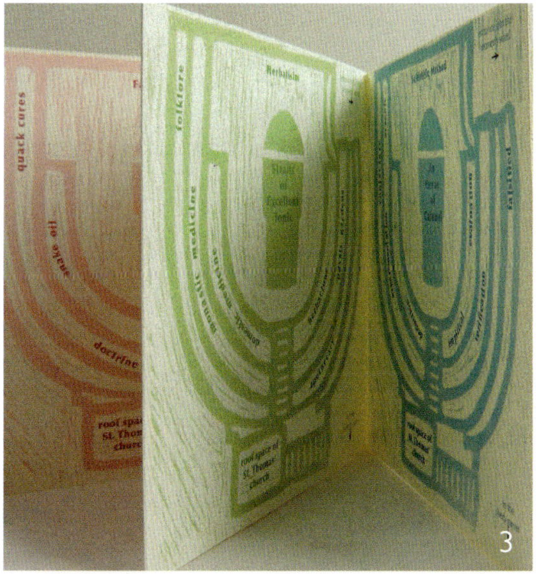

3

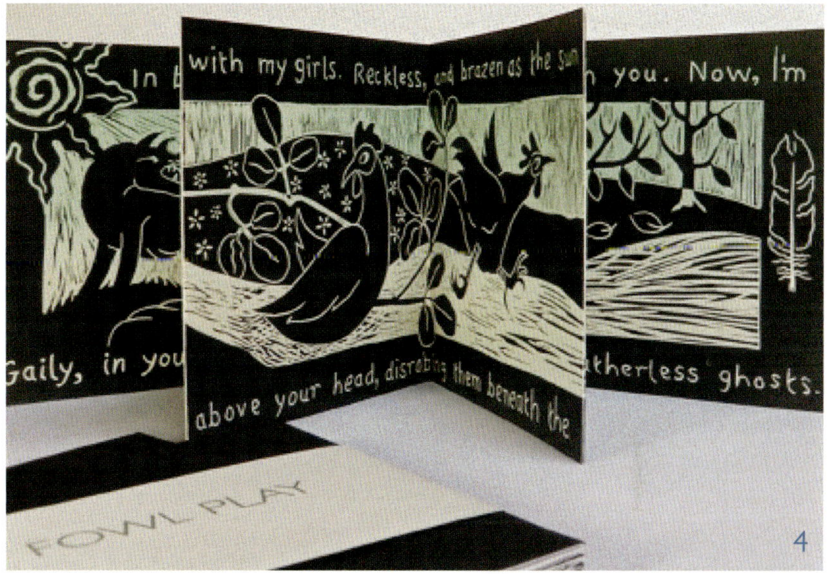

4

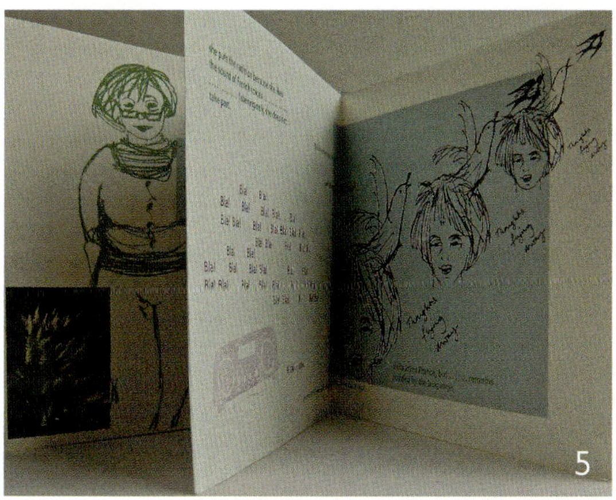
5

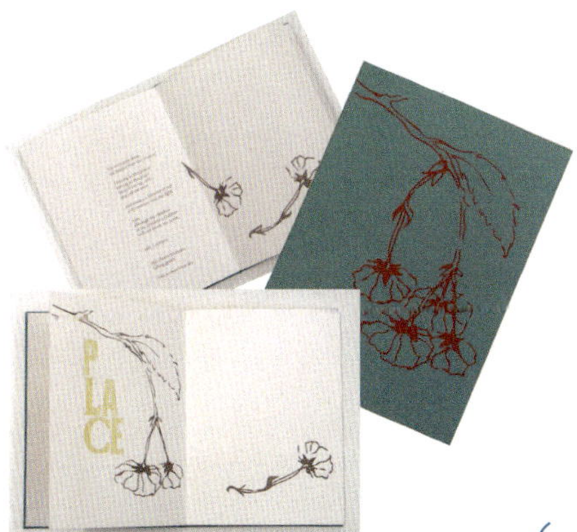

6

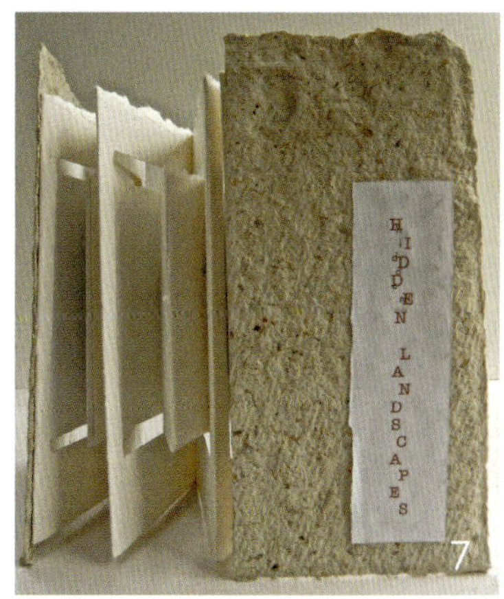

7

Louise Baker

louisepbaker@gmail.com
www.louisepbaker.uk.com

1

Hare and Harp
case 23 x 22 x 4 cm
book 21.5 x 20.5 x 3 cm
Hardcase binding in padded and quilted gold lame, collograph prints on Somerset paper

2

Crow's Nest
26 x 27.5 cm
Japanese style hardcover, lino-cut images on sumi - e Japanese paper, black bookcloth
& Corvidae *13 x15 x 3 cm, linocut and letterpress on handmade paper.*

Louise Baker makes one off books and small editions based on observational drawings from journeys, a specific site or event. The images used are made using various relief print, lino, wood and rubber or intaglio techniques, collographs or etchings printed on size specific handmade, Somerset or Japanese paper. The format, bindings, slip covers or museum cases and sometimes lecterns are integral parts of each completed volume.

Crow's Nest is a set of lino prints each showing a stage from a pair of crows nesting in an ash tree in a Somerset garden to their two chicks fledging.

The Hare and Harp is a series of collograph prints that evolved from an image seen on a fount at Hawkchurch. The book shows the story of the hare finding a harp and returning it to where it was made. The binding is quilted gold lamé on board in a bookcloth bound museum case.

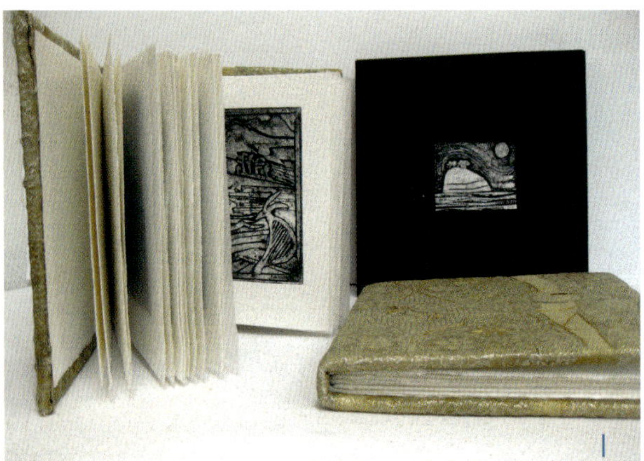

1

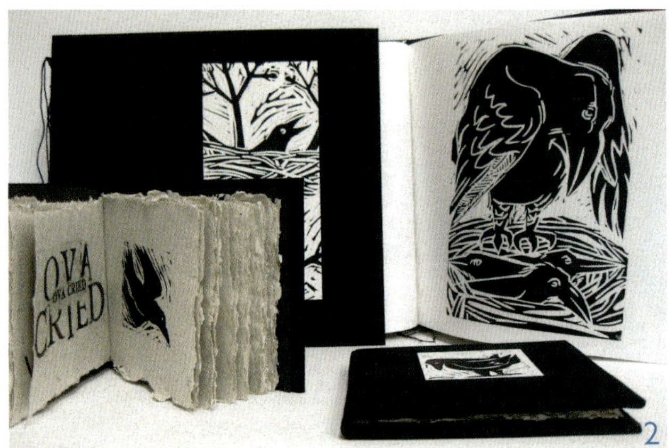

2

Lucy Baxandall

lucybax@yahoo.com
www.lucybaxandall.com

1
Trostbuechlein
Mehr Licht
30 x 14 x 12 cm
Linen and cotton paper, leather, spatula.

2
Trostbuechlein
Map
30 x 12 x 14 cm
Linen and cotton papers, water - colour, ink,

3
Urbs in Horto
(Third State)
17 x 12 cm
Cotton and linen paper, inkjet images, ink.

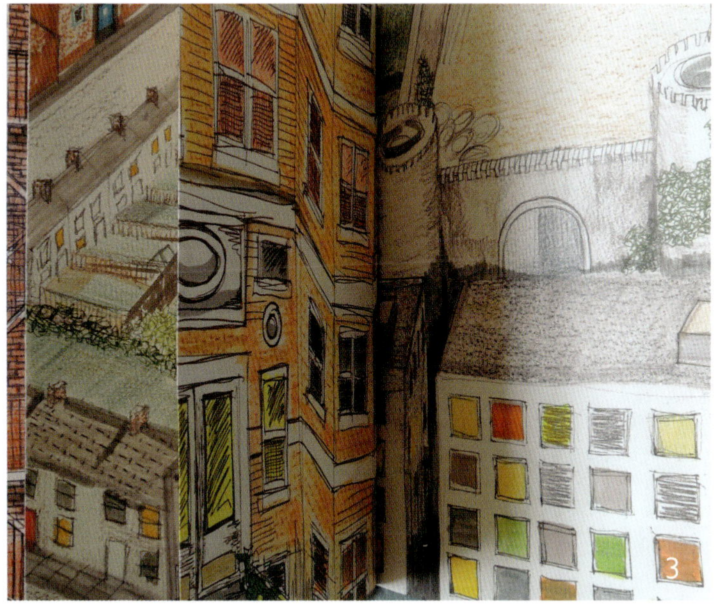
3

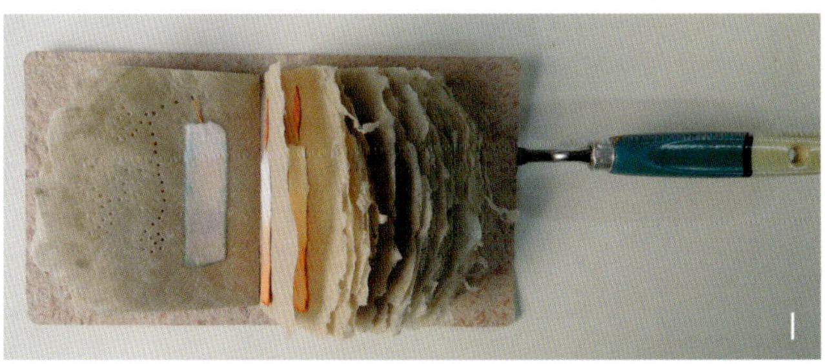
1

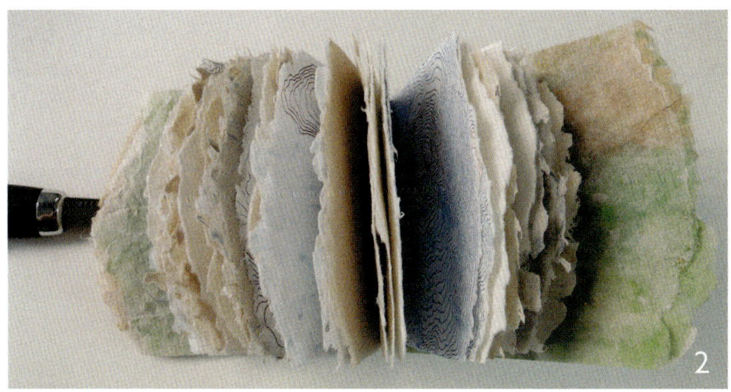
2

Ros Blackmore

rosblackmore8@googlemail.com
www.covetandwhistle.co.uk

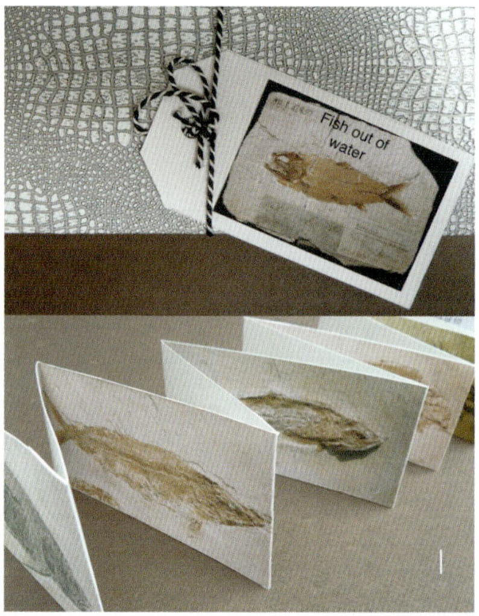

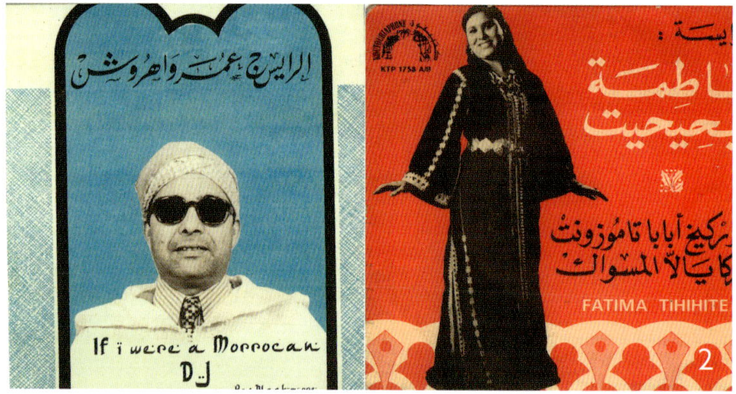

The physicality of making books and the intimacy of reading is exciting. Researching a subject, producing prints, collages, photographs and collecting ephemera becomes an obsession. Binding them all together, allows for these compulsions to be viewed and become accessible to others.

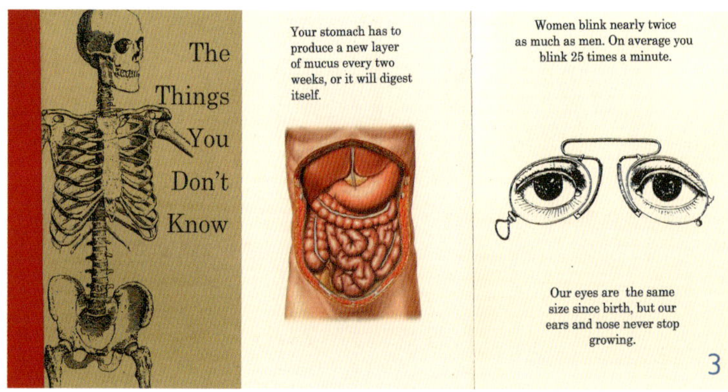

1
Fish out of water
14 x 6.5 cm
Hard cover, concertina book, 12 images

2
If I were a Morrocan DJ
19.5 x 16 cm
16 pages hard cover, Includes 2 CD's

3
The things you don't know
15 x 21.5 cm
Hard cover
10 pages

Bronwen Bradshaw

bronbradshaw@yahoo.com
www.bronwenbradshaw.co.uk

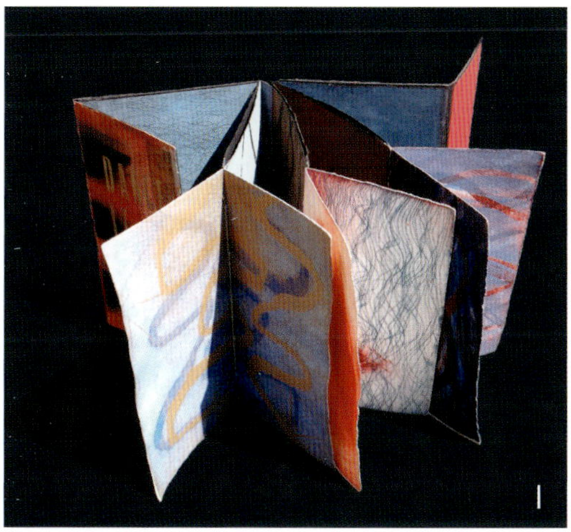

1

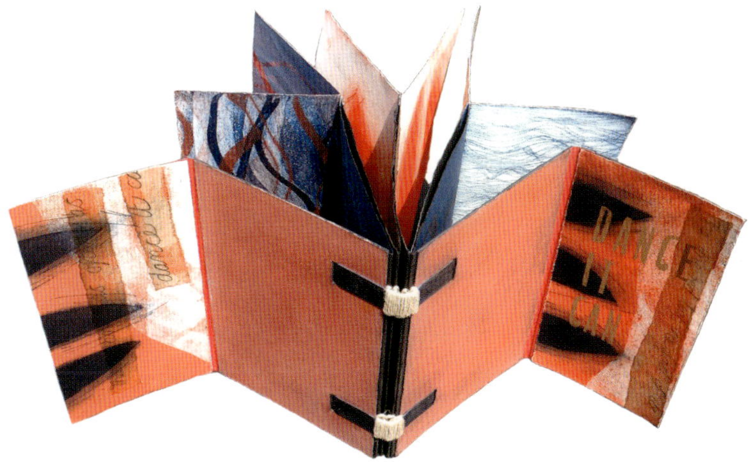

2

1 & 2
Dance it Can
26 x 22 cm
Original etchings
Concertina binding with supported spine sewing, edition of 5 2011

3
Water Snakes
Etchings from 'Dance it Can'
The etchings in this book were inspired by the poetry of Coleridge

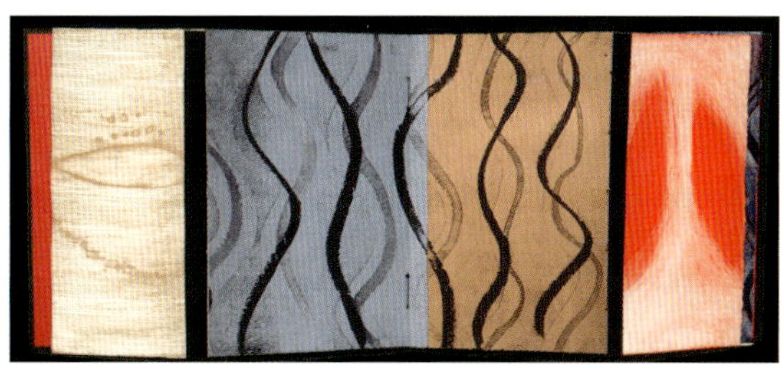

3

Martyn Brewster

martynbrewster@btinternet.com
www.martynbrewster.co.uk

Martyn Brewster is represented by Waterhouse and Dodd Fine Art, London and New York.

1 & 3
Black and White
10 x 60 cm
Woodblock prints, inside and cover.
Edition of 12

2
Covers of four different books
each 20 x 20 cm, silkscreen print.

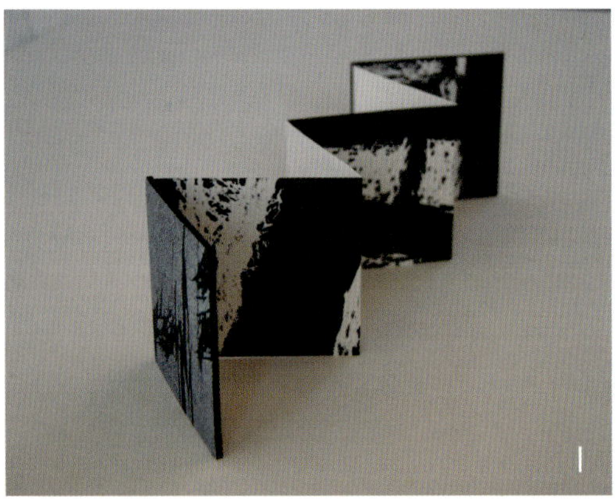

1

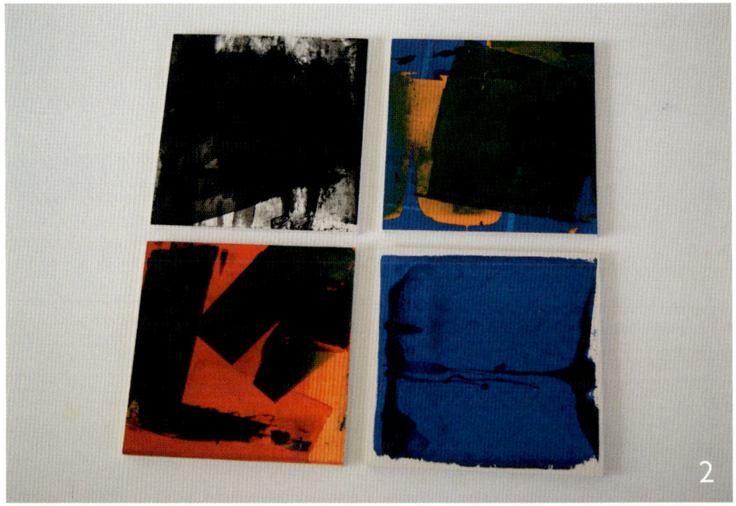

2

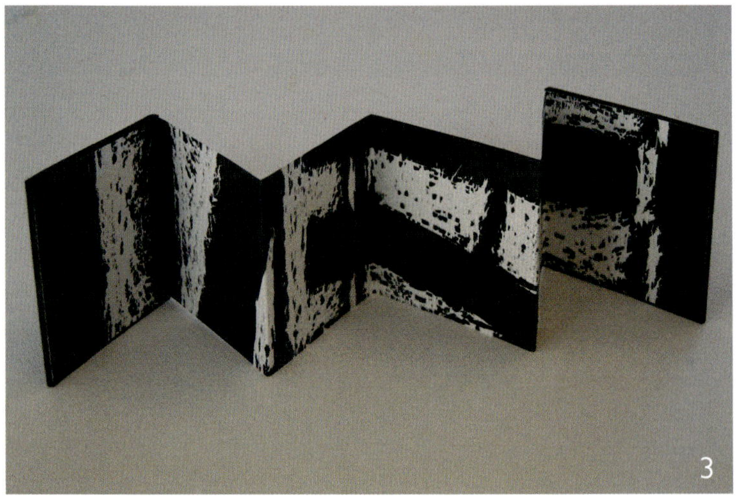

3

4
1st image orange
Concertina book no.10 silkscreen 20 x 120 cm

5
Double page spread, book No 9,
Silkscreen printed, concertina folded

6
Covers of four different books
each 20 x 20 cm Silkscreen print.

7 & 8
Black and White
10 x 60 cm Woodblock print cover, concertina folded. Edition of 12

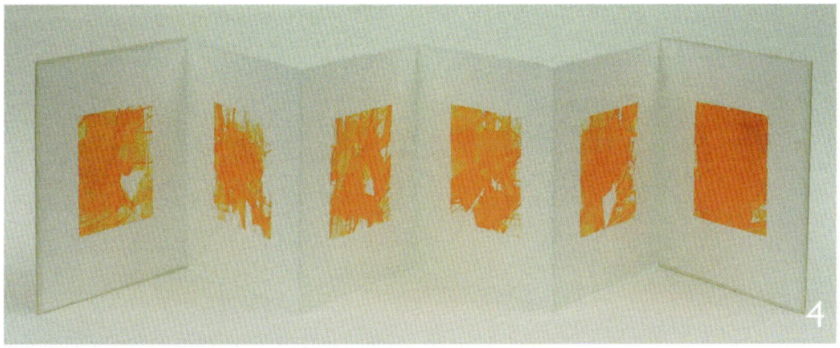
4

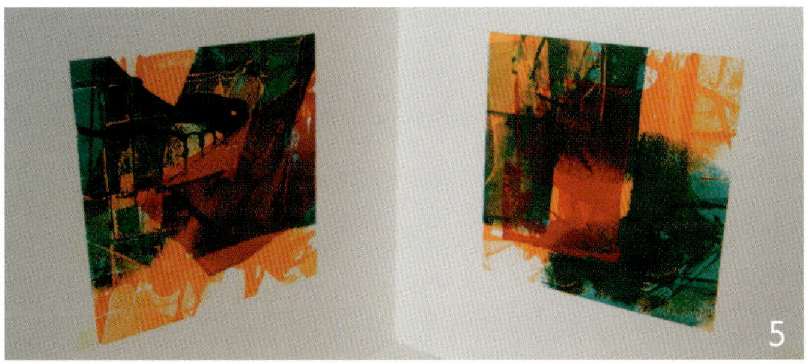
5

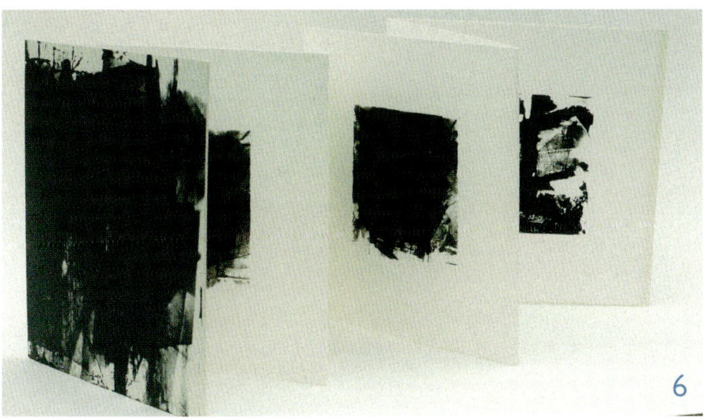
6

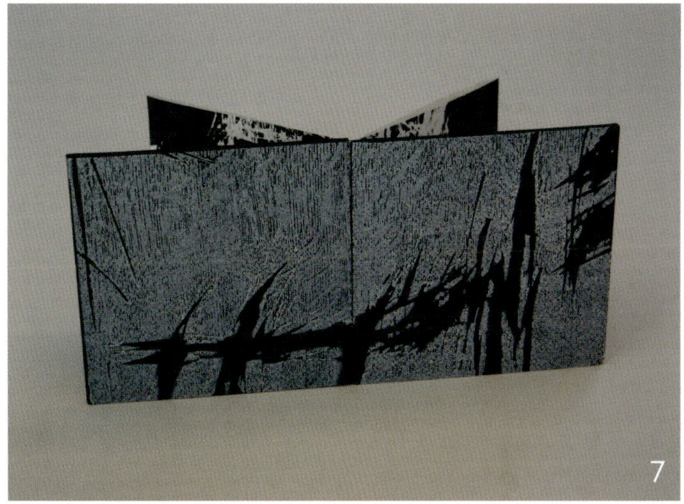
7

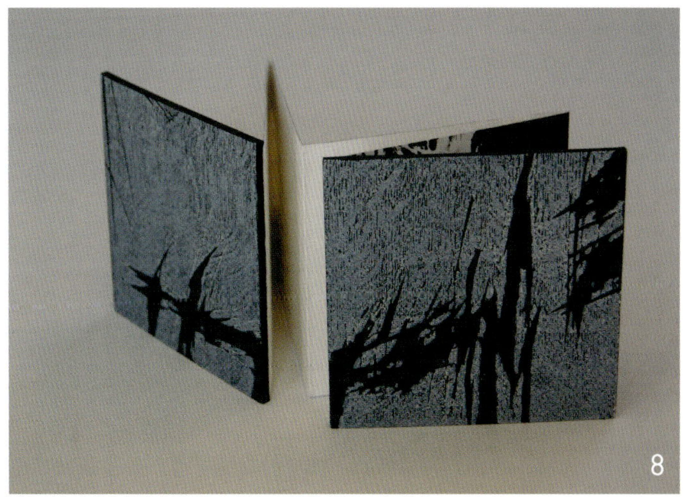
8

Jennifer Bruce

jennifer.rose.bruce@gmail.com
www..jenniferrosebruce.com.

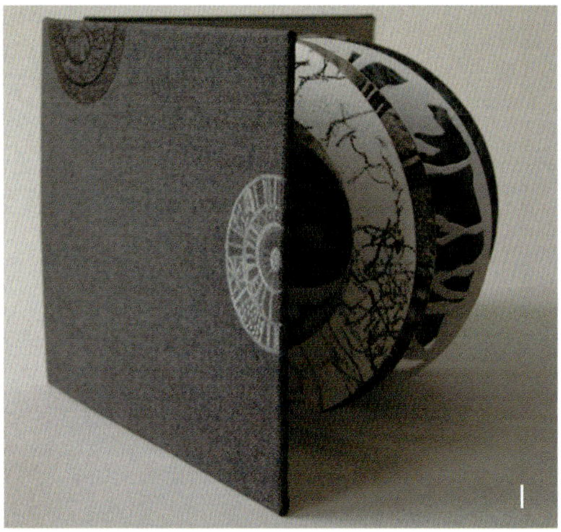

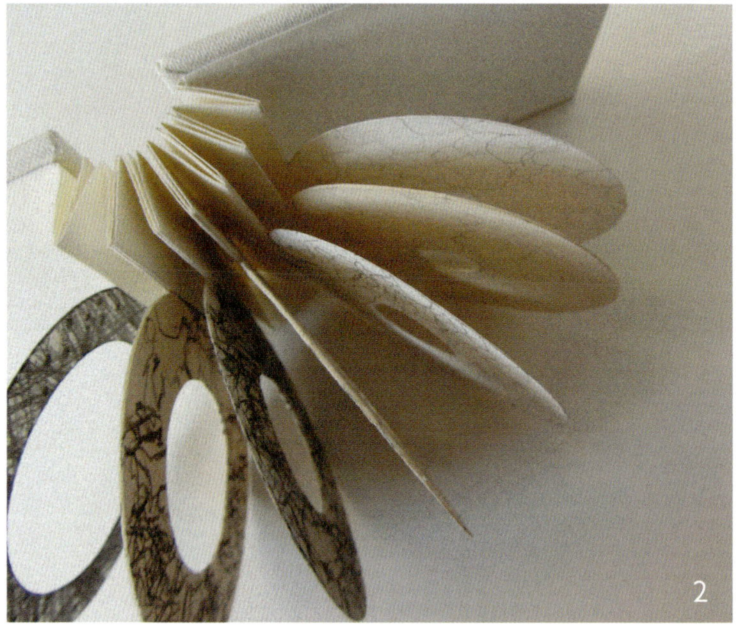

1
The Only Way Out is Through A/P1
10 x 8 cm
Paper, mixed media, greyboard, bookcloth, thread

2
The Only Way Out is Through A/P2
8 x 6 cm
Paper, pencil, greyboard, bookcloth, thread

3
The Only Way Out is Through A/P2 (detail)
8 x 6 cm
Paper, pencil, greyboard, bookcloth, thread

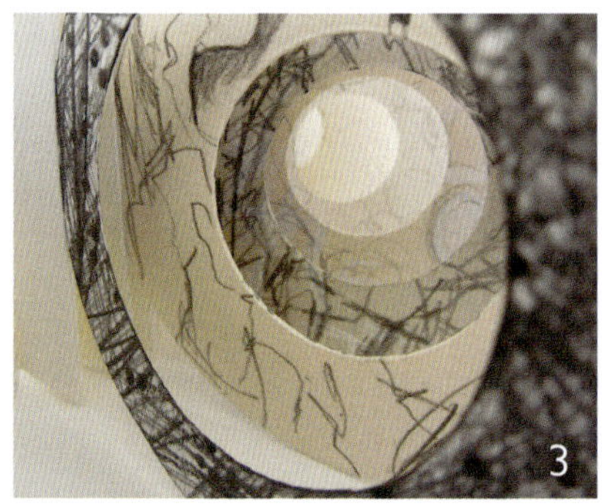

Sarah Bryant
Big Jump Press

sarahherrickbryant@gmail.com
www.bigjumppress.com

Sarah Bryant, who operates under the name Big Jump Press, designs and produces letterpress-printed artist's books in editions ranging in size from ten to 100 copies. Her work can be found in dozens of collections including The Yale Arts Library, The Houghton Library at Harvard University, The New York Public Library and The Darling Bio-medical Library at UCLA. Big Jump Press books incorporate analytical imagery, reference material, and innovative binding structures. They use diagrammatic language, such as the periodic table, population data sets, and cutaway cross sections, to set up complex investigations of more human themes.

Bryant has taught bookbinding and letterpress printing courses for a number of universities in the United States, her country of origin. She currently lives in Brighton and teaches workshops and short courses in the south of England.

1
Biography
22 x 14 x 2 cm
Letterpress printed on Zerkall paper in an edition of 75

2
Fond
18.5 x 11.5 x 1.5 cm
Letterpress printed on Zerkall paper in an edition of 75

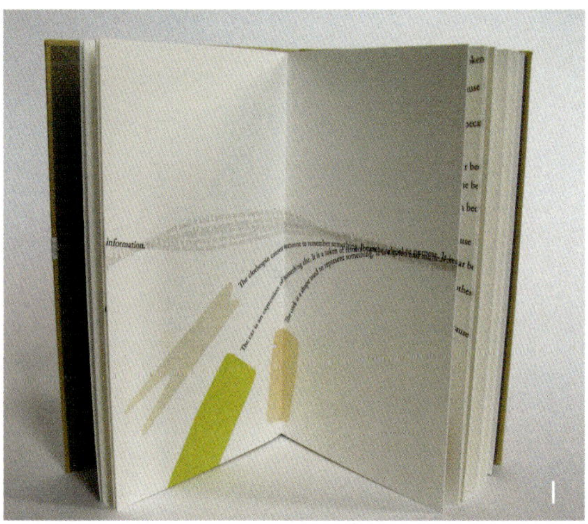

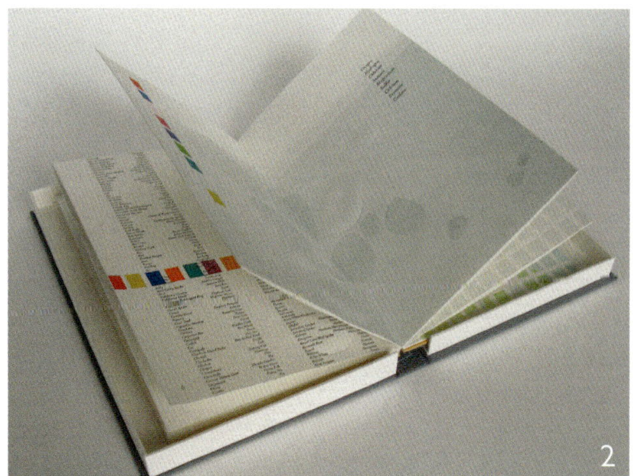

Miranda Campbell
Bookspells

bookspells@gmail.com
www.bookspells.com

1 & 2

Flight

11 x 30 cm Ivy, bird feathers, artists' paper 130 gsm, concertina folded, wire bird cage

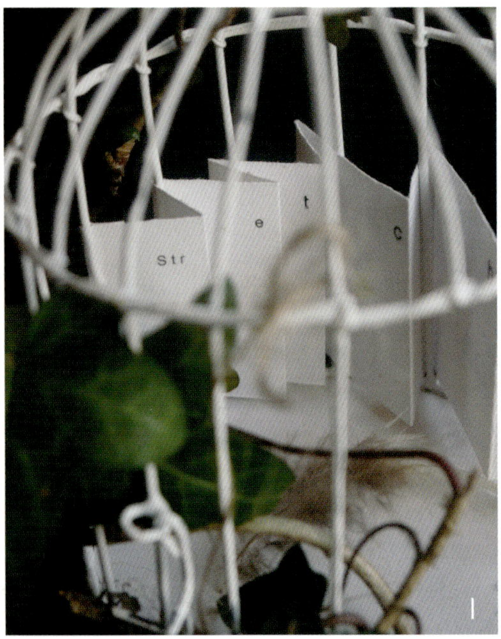

A good story collapses time, weaving together fragmented voices with contemporary images that fire the imagination and evoke strong feelings. Book art adds that exciting dimension to storytelling for Miranda Campbell, allowing her to combine language and emotion with texture and structure.

Miranda specialises in beautiful handmade books and contemporary book art, incorporating original narrative, traditional bookbinding techniques, natural materials and decorative stitching. Her books are influenced by life's rich tapestry, and the delicate threads that bind us to each other and shape our affinity for space and place.

Miranda has an MA (Distinction) in 'Art, Design and The Book' from The Minories in Colchester. She is a member of the Society of Bookbinders, the Designer Bookbinders and the Fine Press Book Association. She is editor of 'Single Fold', the newsletter for the East Anglian Region of the Society of Bookbinders.

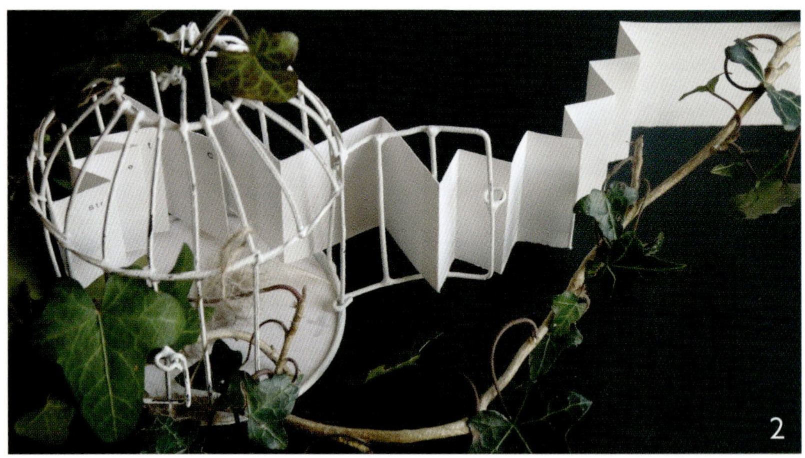

3 & 6
Keep out & detail
12 x 22 cm
Eucalyptus bark, paper birch bark, handmade paper, silver wire, embossed leaves

4 & 5
Scattered words
21.5 x 70 cm
African calf skin, Arches 185 gsm, concertina folded, handcut footprints, original narrative

7
Handmade notebook
7.5 x 9 cm
Long stitch limp leather binding, decorative beadwork, artists' paper 130 gsm

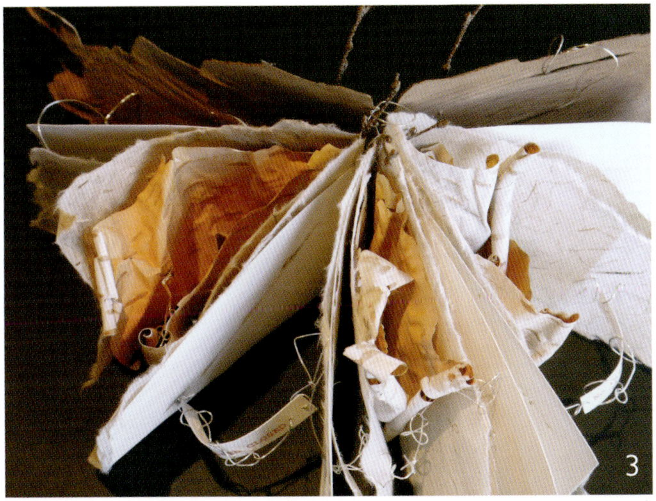
3

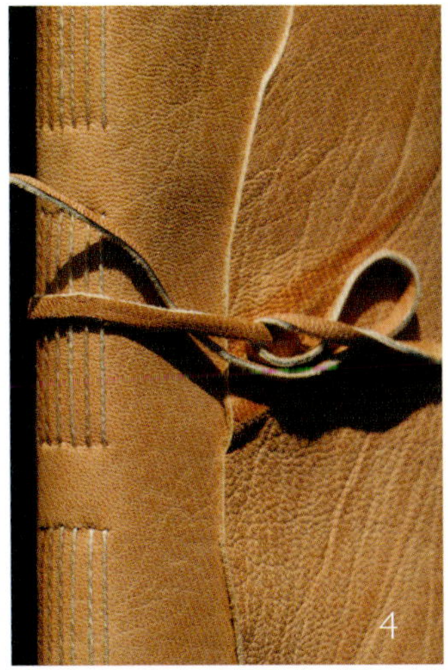
4

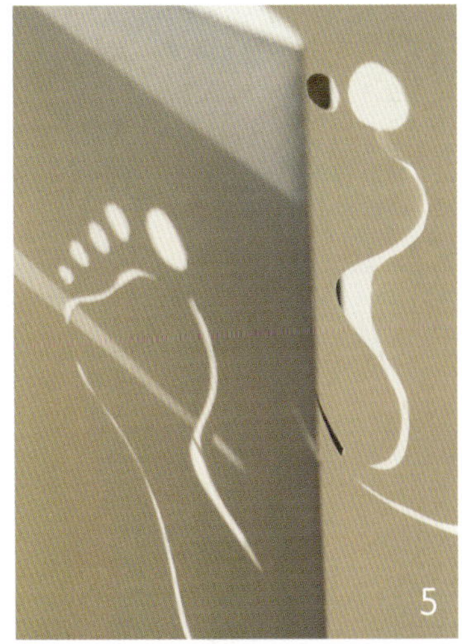
5

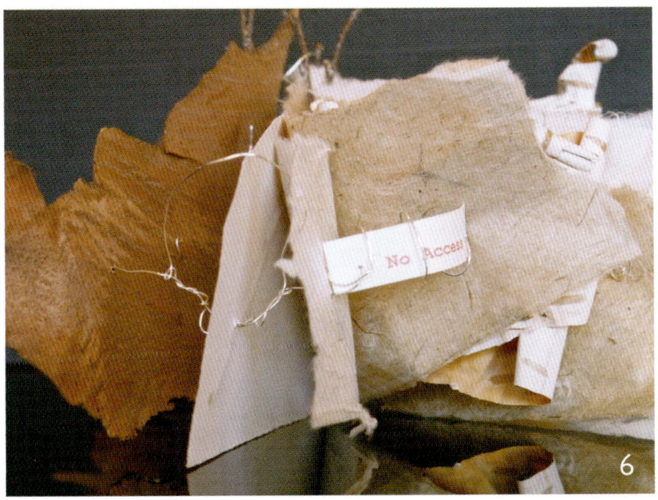

6

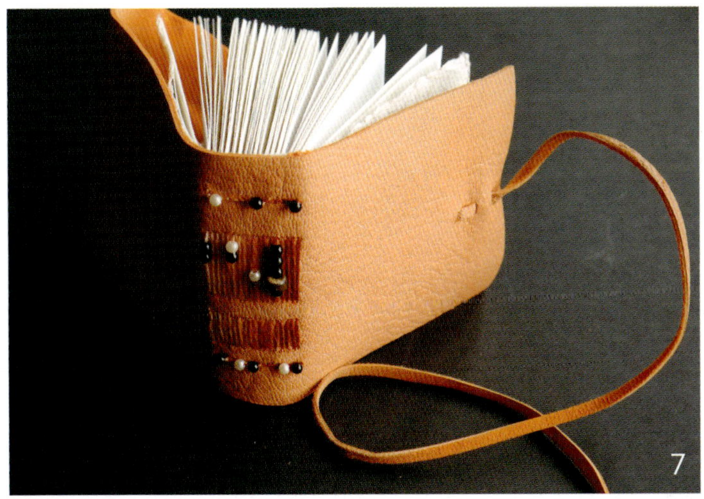
7

The Celtic Cross Press

Limited edition books printed letterpress on fine paper
Poetry & short stories, with original illustrations
Books still in print are available from:
www.celticcrosspress.com

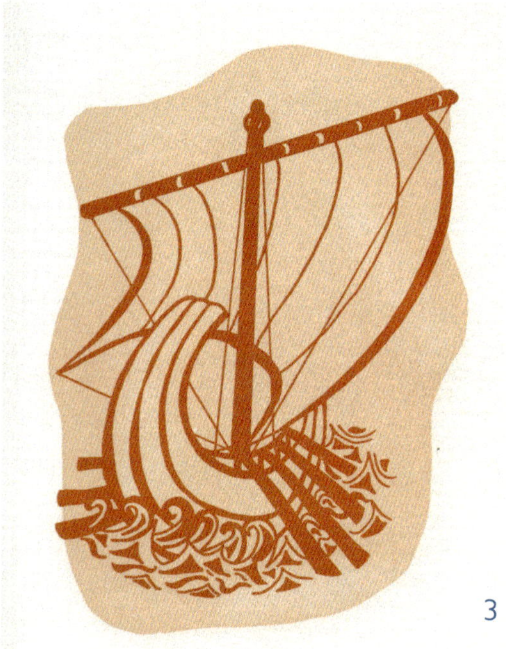

3

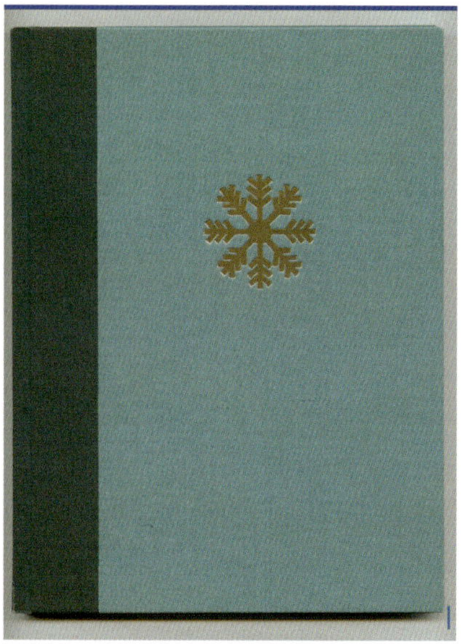

1

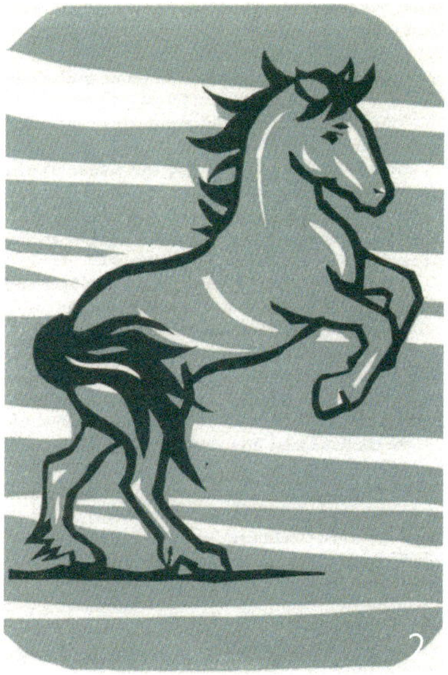

2

1 & 2
Christmas Tales' by George Mackay Brown
cover & lino-cut

3
'Odysseus: the ships' Poems by George Mackay Brown
drawing

Christopher Churcher

chris@christopherchurcher.co.uk
christopherchurcher.co.uk

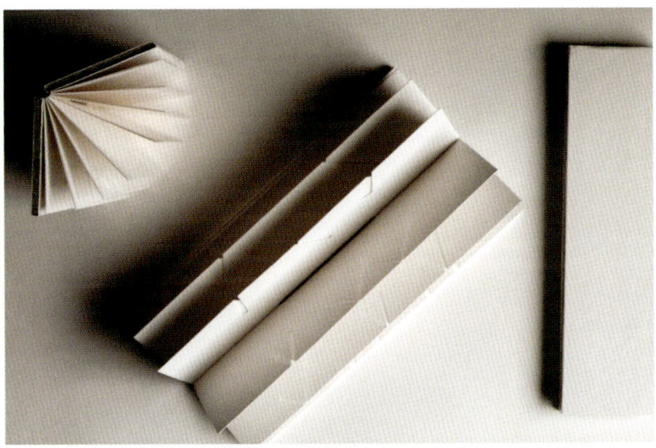

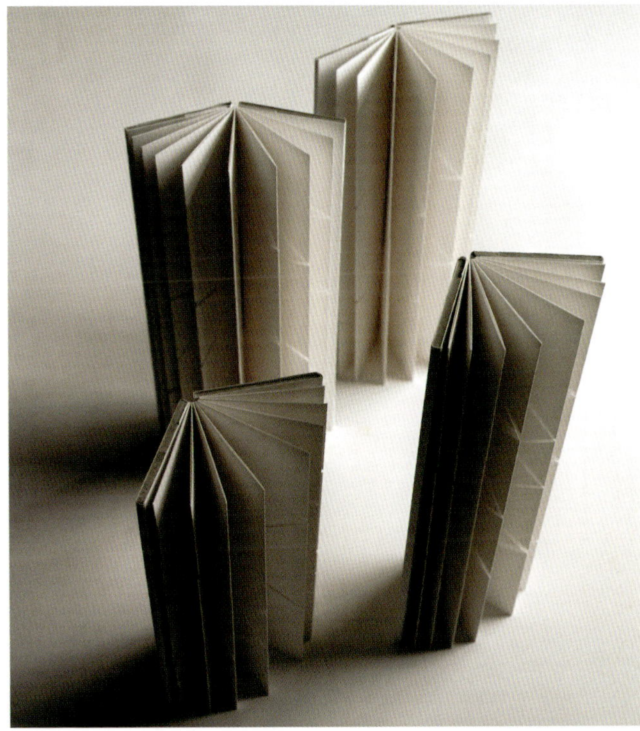

Automatic Paper
15 x 4 x 1 cm   Paper and Card

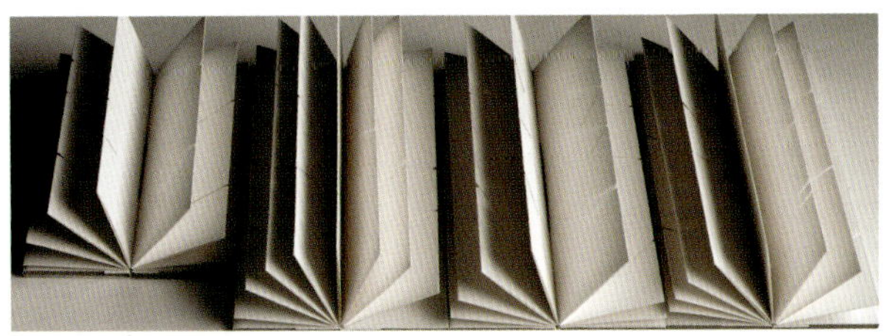

Bronwen Coe

tulips@bronwencoe.co.uk
www.bronwencoe.com

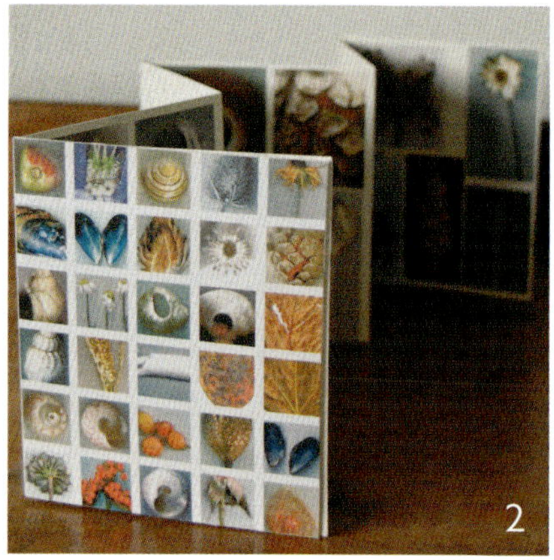

1
Timeless Garden
16 x 83 cm
300gsm hot pressed cartridge. Handprinted & graphite pencil, concertina folded

2 & 3
Ephemerata
66 x 14 cm
300gsm hot pressed cartridge & light cartridge, concertina folded

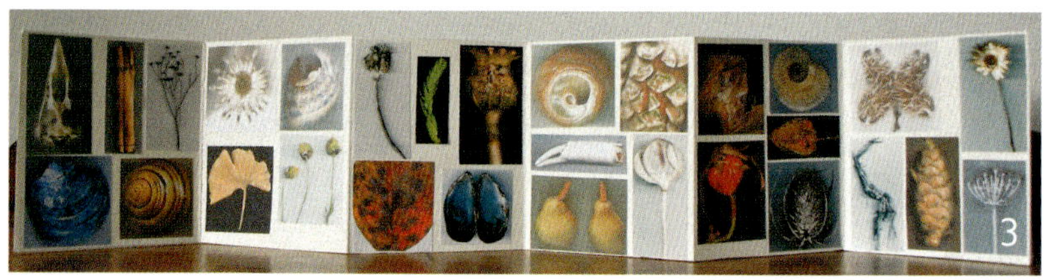

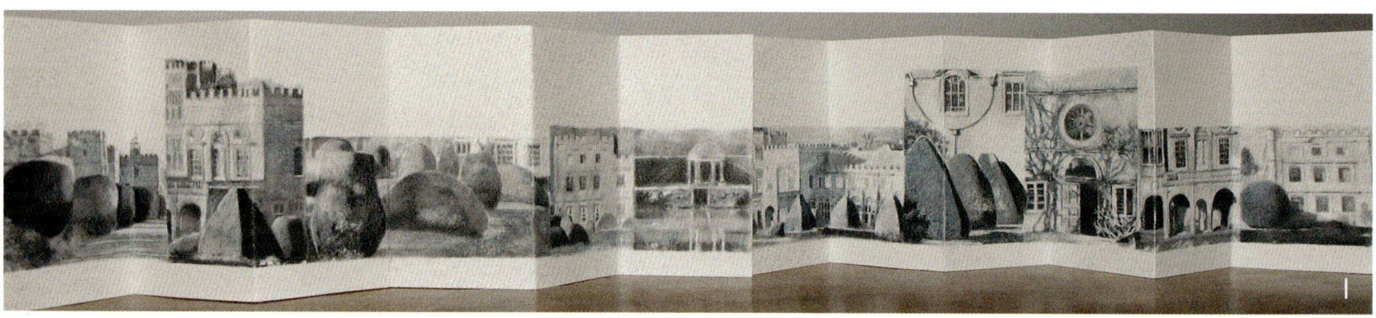

Sue Corr

suecorr@btinternet.com
www.suecorr.com

Sue Corr's tactile palm sized books are intriguing objects. Their intimacy reflects her close connection with nature and a desire to draw attention to the minutiae of the world around us. Folded, embossed, stitched and dotted with text typed on an old Eastern bloc typewriter the 'Snow Book' is a culmination of work started on a residency in Quebec City and completed in the UK.

For further information and to view or buy beautiful hand made books please visit www.suecorr.com

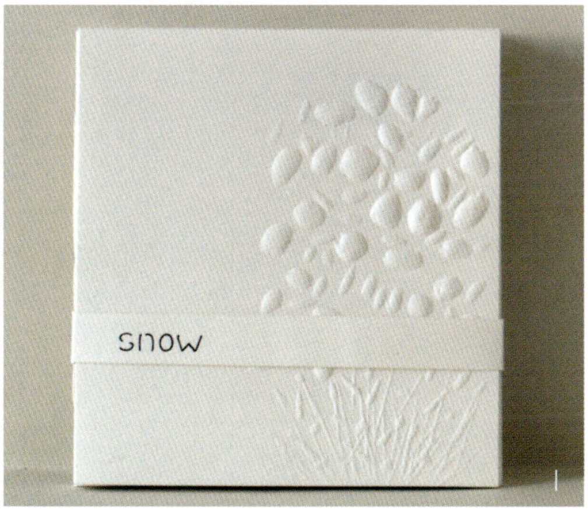

1

Snow book (2013)

9.7 x 10.4 cm opening out to 96.5 cm

Folded concertina book embossed and printed using various techniques with minimal stitching

limited edition tbc

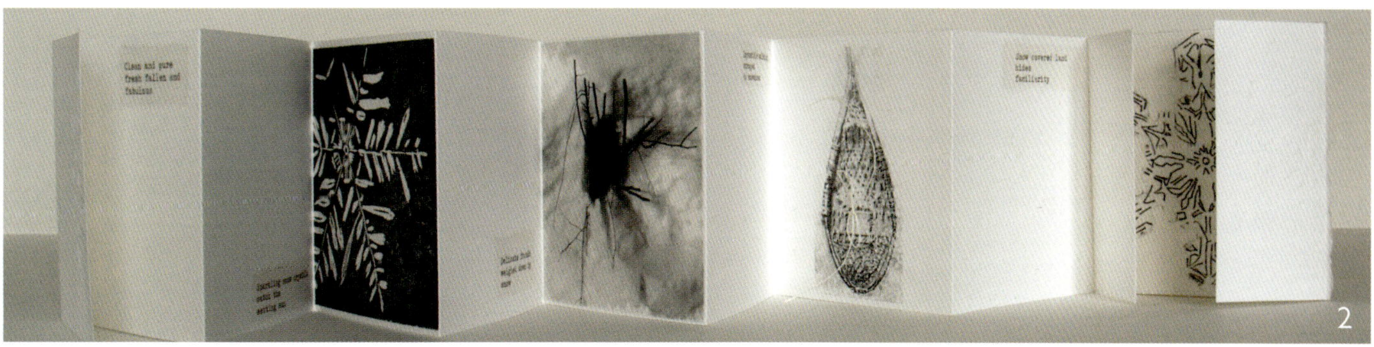

2

Larissa Cox
Boundless Bookbindery

coxlarissa@hotmail.com
www.larissacox.com

From the instant you turn the first page, you're completely immersed in Larissa Cox's fantastic miniature world: the lattice of tree trunks and architectural structures appears to recede into a nearly infinite depth, and the further through the book you go, the deeper you penetrate into the Cathedral, as one of the works is called. In other works one sees doors opening onto overgrown gardens, or the bookshelf of a witch, or an eery subterranean street-scene: secret worlds hidden within books. She calls these mysterious paper worlds 'collage books,' created using a combination of self-taught collage and book-binding techniques, not to mention meticulous and highly skillful cutting work. She has focused on developing this innovative format since 2001.

Born in 1973 in Bath, England, Larissa has lived and worked in Vienna, Austria, since 2000.

1
Garden
25.5 x 29 cm
closed. Handbound book with 3D hand-cut collage - both images.

2
Path
25.5 x 32 cm
closed

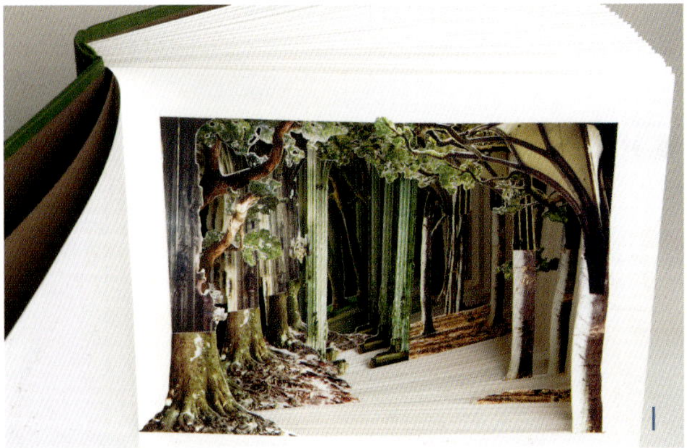

1

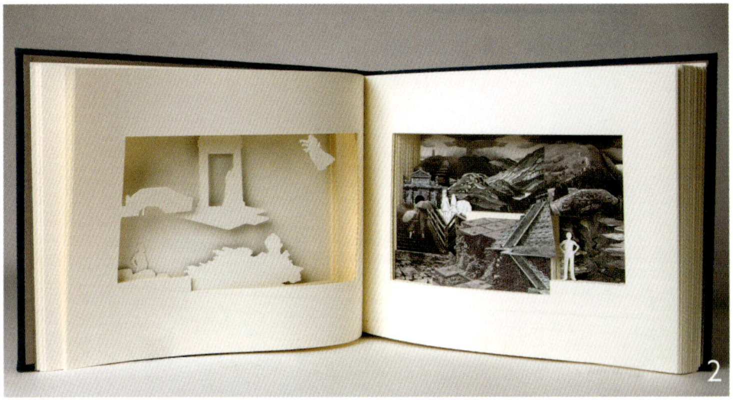

2

3
Cathedral
26 x 30 cm closed. Handbound book with 3D hand-cut collage - all images

4
Larissa Cox with her work Cathedral

5
Witch
25.5 x 36 cm closed

6
Street
25.5 x 32 cm closed

7
Raven
23 x 27 cm closed

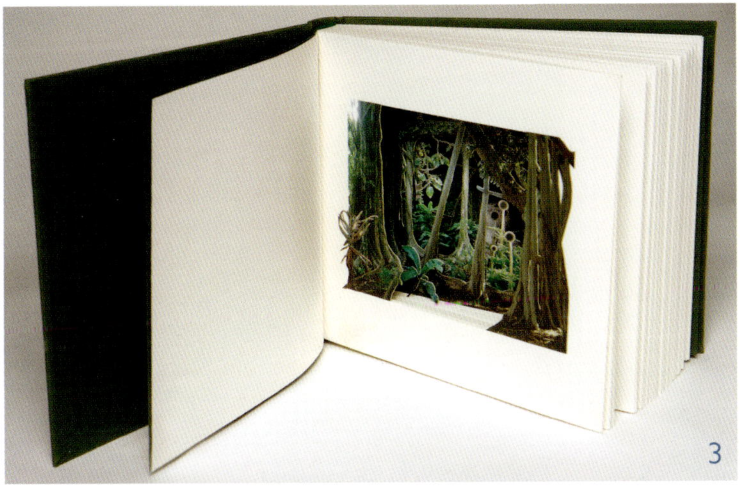

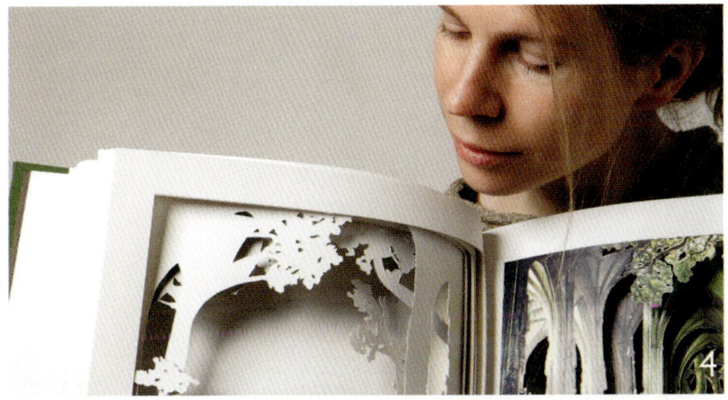

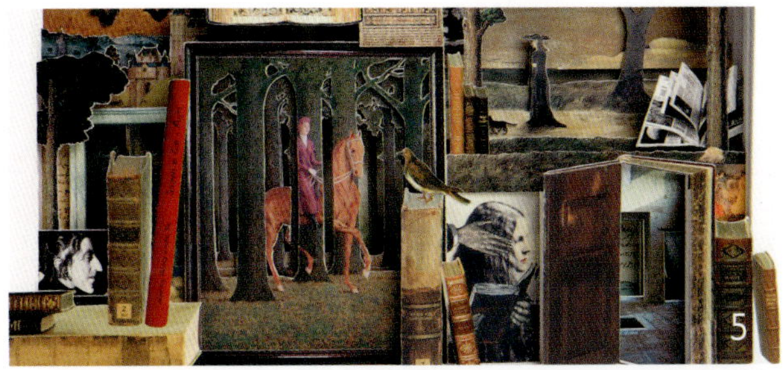

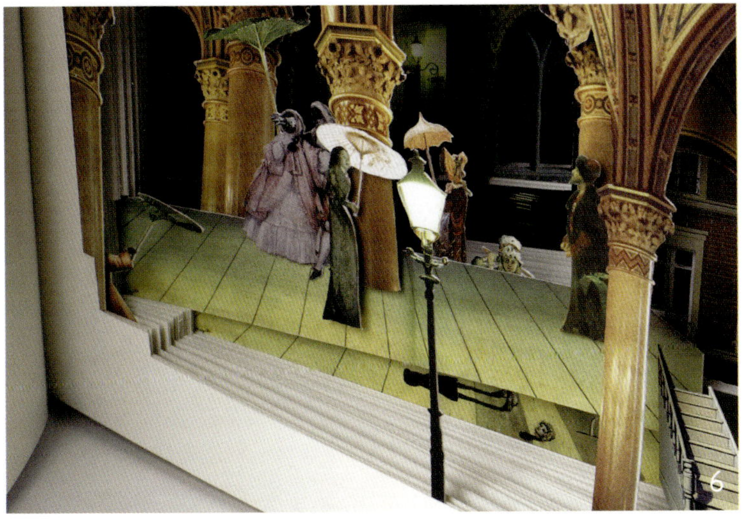

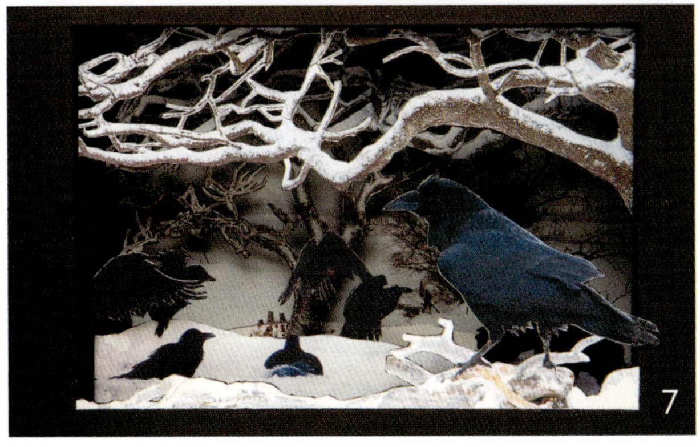

Penny Cuthbert

penny@dodlaw.co.uk
www.pennycuthbert.co.uk

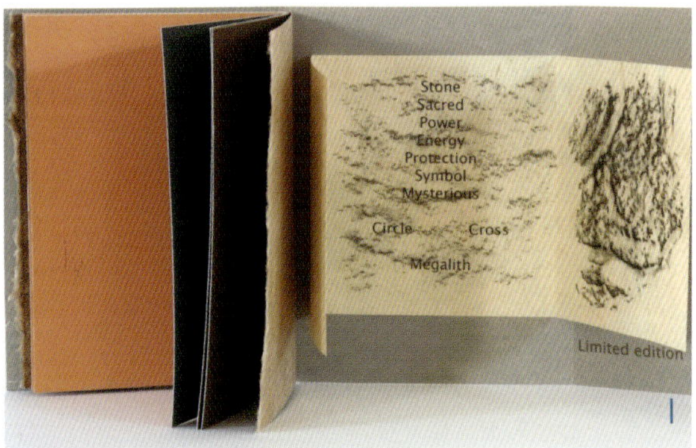

1

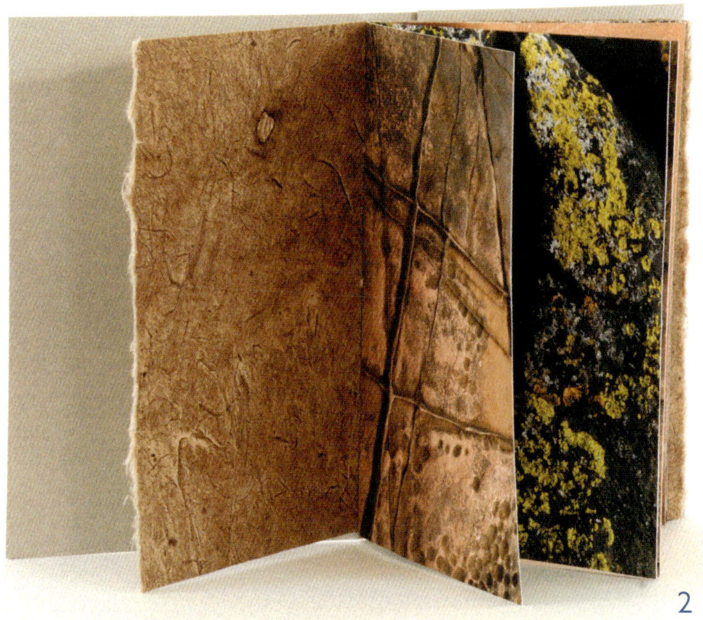

2

1 & 2

Stone
15.2 x 11.5 cm
Canson paper. Handmade paper. Double sided photographic paper inkjet printed. Pamphlet.

3

Refuge
10 x 7 x 70 cm
Double sided photographic paper. Inkjet printed, concertina folded. Handmade paper packet.

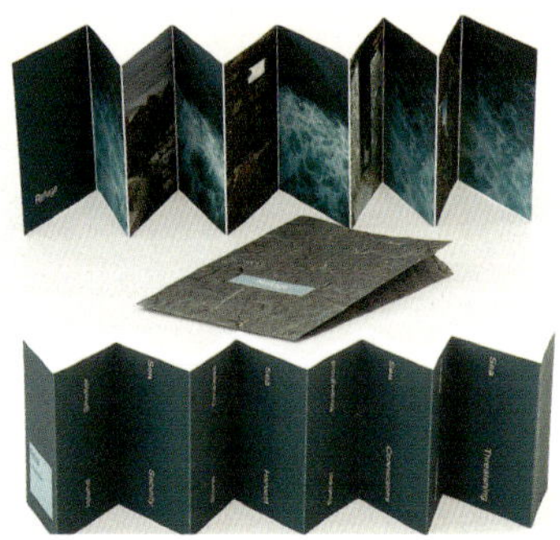

3

ABCD (cont'd)

ABCD at Dove Studios
cm@craftgalleries.co.uk
Also please see pages 9, 37, & 49

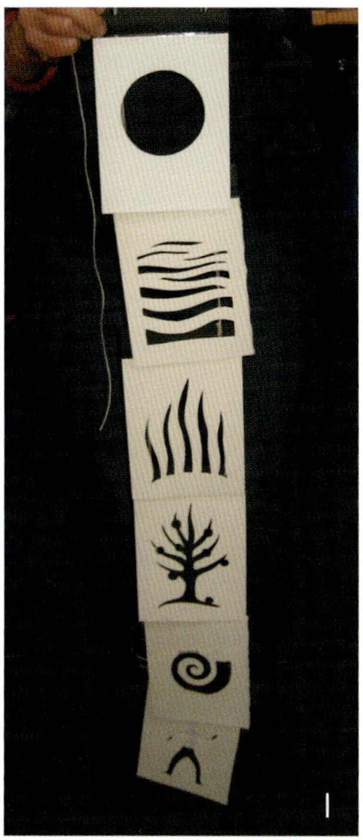

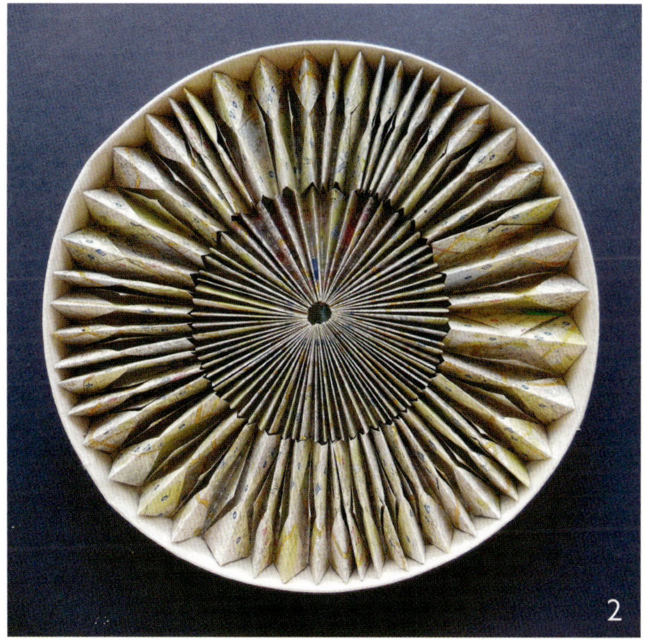

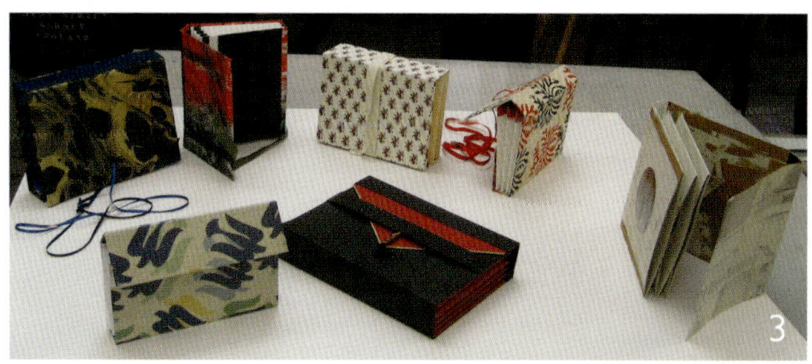

1 Hanging book
by Pat Wolseley

2 A - Z Mapping Book
by Karen Young

3 Selection of
Container Books by
group members

Susan Cutts

susan@susancutts.com
www.susancutts.com

Susan Cutts is a sculptor working with her own handmade paper. Her artist books are based on a little known Chinese tradition called zhen xian bao. These intricately folded and decorated books are used by needlewomen to store the tools of their trade and as well as passing technique from mother to daughter.

Susan has used this basic 'book' construction to create personal memory books or as they are more commonly known 'folded secrets'. She says of the Chinese books 'the initial attraction was the function of the books and coming from a long line of milliners and dressmakers I appreciate how important traditional skills are within the family structure'. As a hand papermaker working with traditional European equipment and techniques Susan is able to create and use papers made from indigenous and oriental fibres.

1
Secret Rose (inner detail)
20 x 21 cm
Text photocopied onto own handmade gampi paper. Traditional folding techniques

2
20 x 21 cm
images photocopied onto dyed gampi. Traditional folding techniques

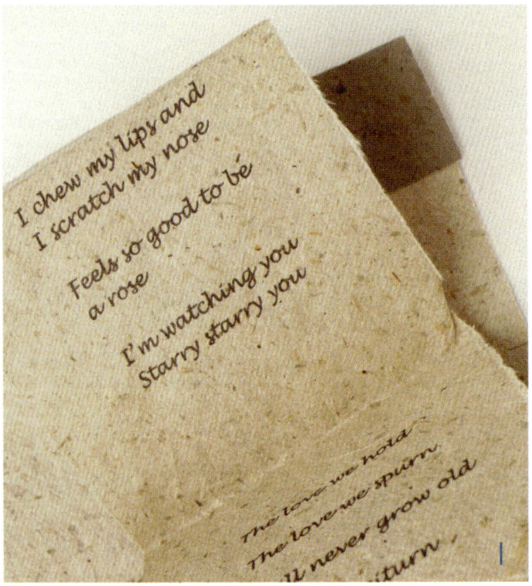

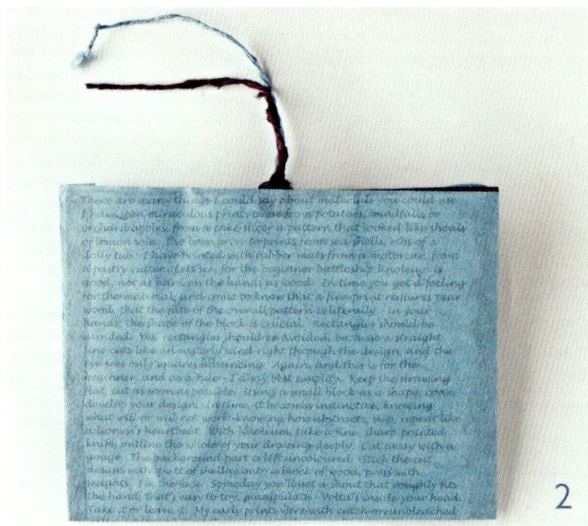

3
Secret Rose (cover)
20 x 21 cm
Images photocopied onto own handmade gampi paper. Traditional folding techniques

4 & 5
Secret Rose (inner detail)
20 X 21 cm
Images photocopied onto own handmade gampi paper. Traditional folding techniques

6 & 7
Hannah (inner detail)
20 x 21cm
Images photocopied onto dyed gampi paper. Traditional folding techniques

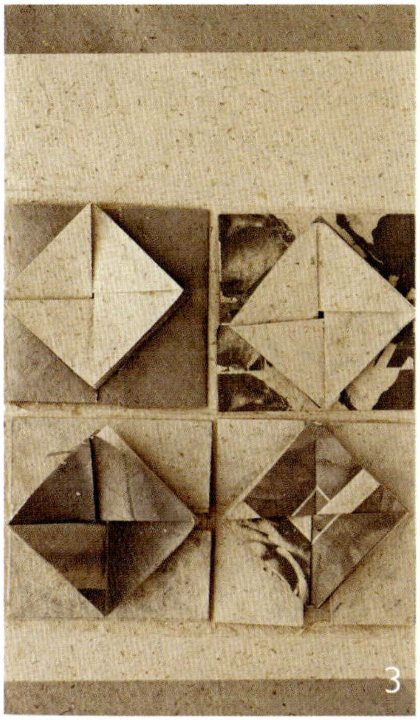
3

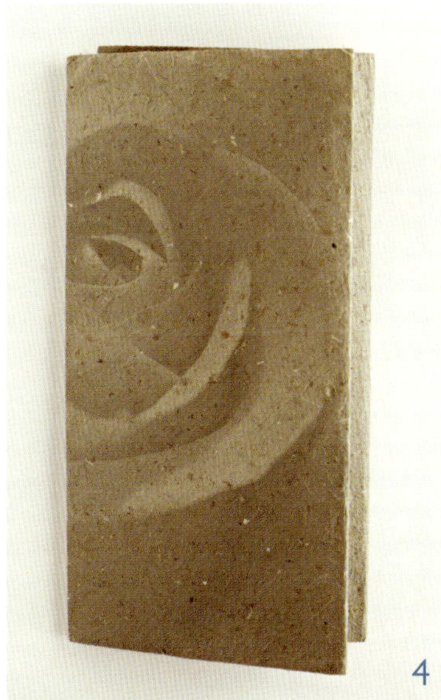
4

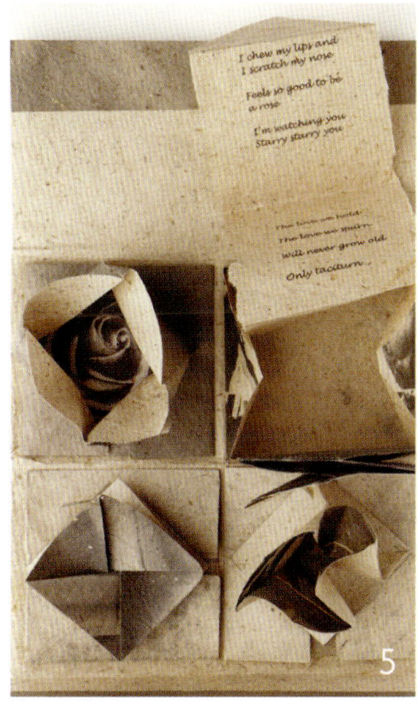

5

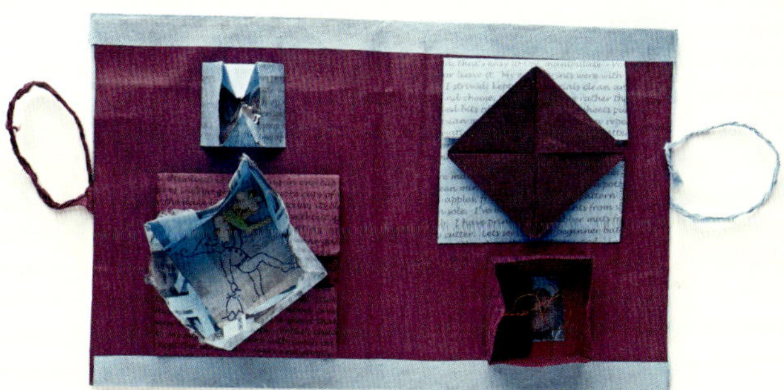
6

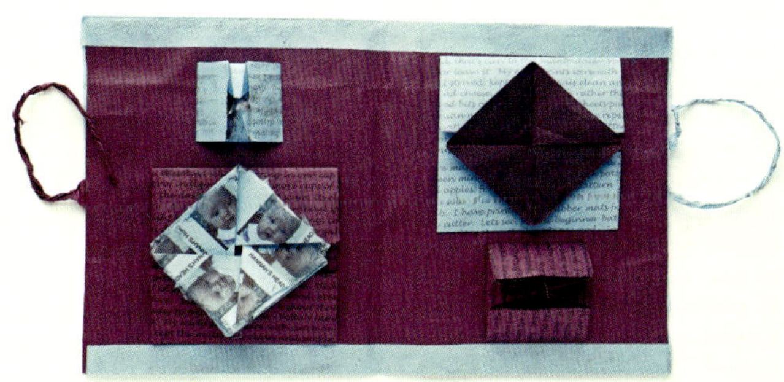
7

Theresa Easton

theresa_easton@yahoo.co.uk
http://theresaeaston.wordpress.com

The Principles of Divergence references Darwin's research into Natural Selection in his book 'On the Origin of Species' 1859. Darwin's detailed and methodical presentation of the animal kingdom provides a wealth of inspiration for Easton's interpretation in the form of a suitcase. The medium of print-making and techniques in making artist's books provides Easton with a fluid connection between idea and object. The suitcase acts as a metaphor and forms part of The Book Apothecary, a travelling museum of artist's books.

Artists' Books provide an analogue platform for Easton's printmaking skills and the opportunity to develop international projects such as The Sunderland Book Project.

The Principles of Divergence
70 x 40 x 30 cm
Re-cycled suitcase, handmade books, found objects and printed glass.

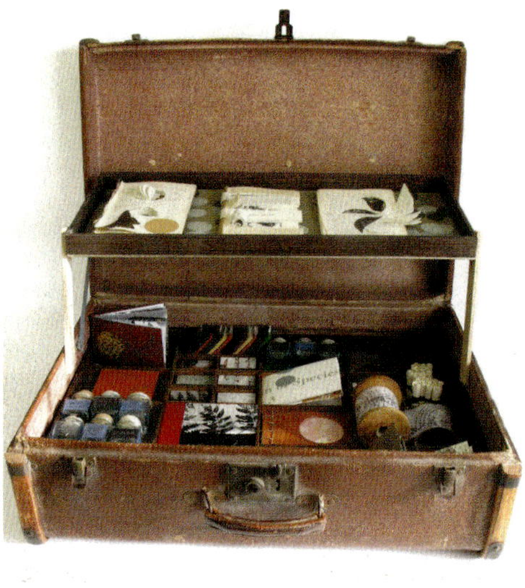

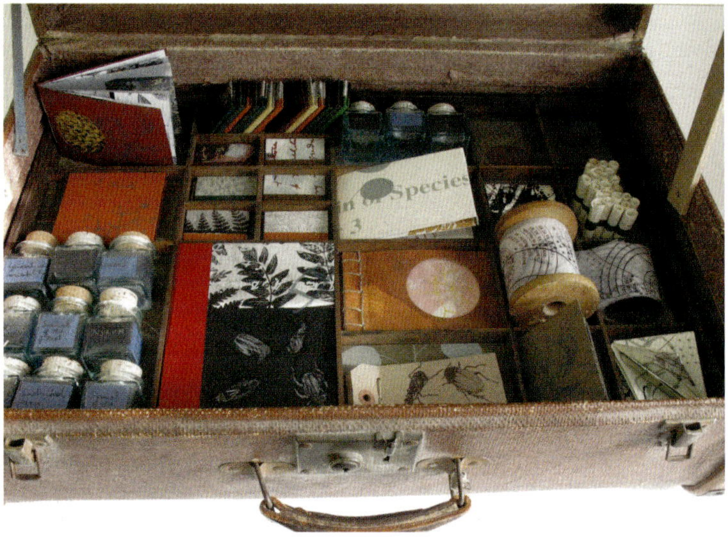

ABCD (cont'd)

ABCD at Dove Studios
cm@craftgalleries.co.uk
Also please see pages 9, 33 & 49

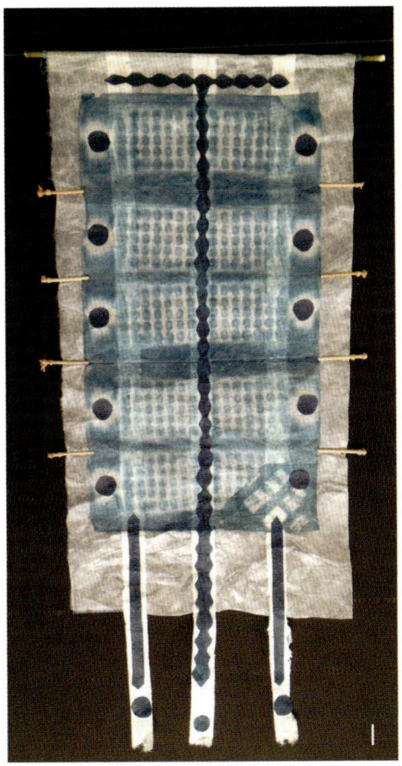

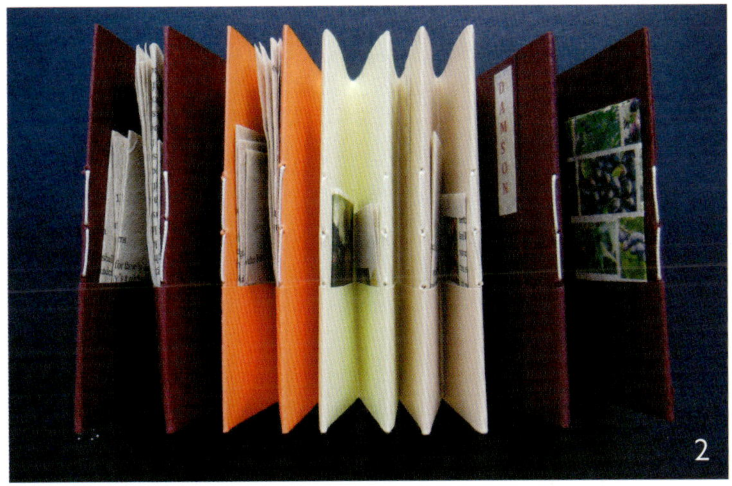

1 Mapping
by Jane Paterson

2 Found
by Karen Young

3 Given
by Karen Young

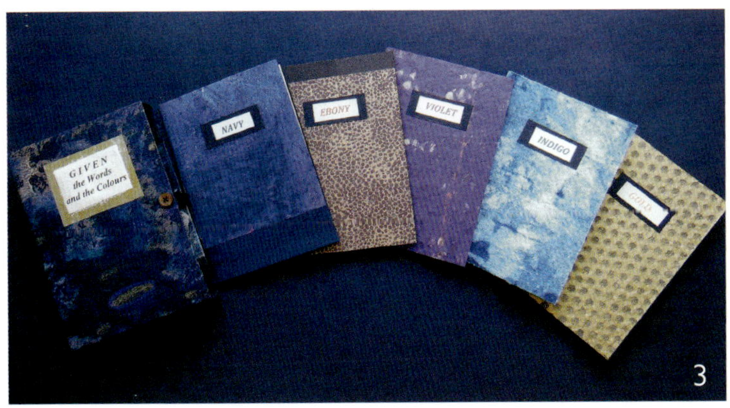

Cath Fairgrieve
Pressing Publications

cathfairgrieve@aol.com

Cath Fairgrieve's artists' books address everyday rituals and social interactions about home and community, where nuances of change and loss are continual. She is fascinated by artefacts in museums where the formalisation of time contrasts to the ad-hock nature of actual life, and by our human compulsion to 'collect stuff' as a means of identifying self.

She works across discipline boundaries, combining traditional processes with new technologies. Drawing provides a creative impulse and is often the resolution of an idea, whilst the book format 'draws in' the viewer through reading. Language structures such as idioms and prepositions or expressions of slang and proverbs are often incorporated. Books themselves are commonplace, hiding behind covers, demanding time for contemplation - but they are also evocative containers for experience. In her books she hopes to capture human commonality through personal narratives.

1
Only sometimes I am round
24.5 x 10.5 cm
Hand drawn and typed on lined copy paper, concertina gussets, grey cloth bound

2
Collectanea
10 x 12.5 cm
Enamelled copper with decals, concertina bound with red stitch

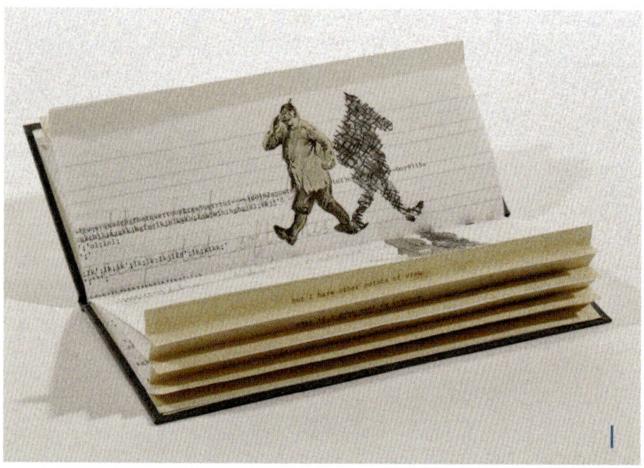

1

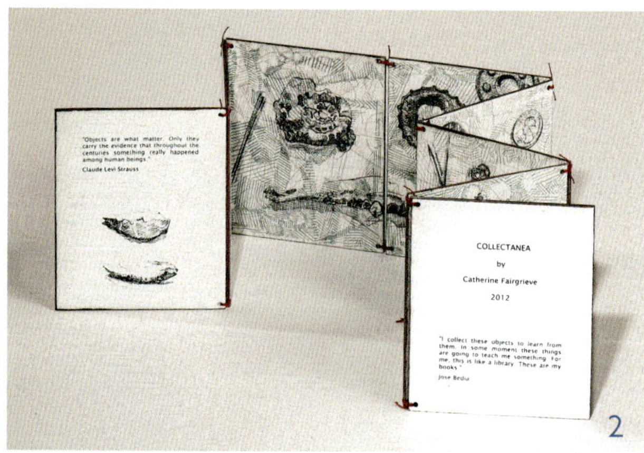

2

3
DIY Manual
39.5 x 29.5 cm
Screen printed on smooth Somerset satin, green cloth - bound with red tooling

4
Library of Lost Books Project 'Stuckey Lean Collectanea'
27 x 20.5 cm
Altered book with laser cut proverbs and screen printed text and images on japanese paper. Re-bound original cover with grey cloth spine and tooling

5
Hold
76 x 55 x 69 cm
Laser etched 19th century oak table with text and mulberry leaf image, one leg sawn short and propped up with a copy of Ovid's 'Metamorphosis'

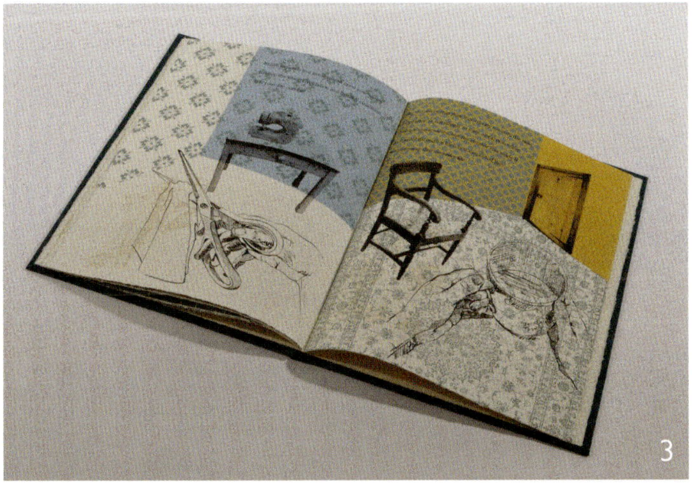

3

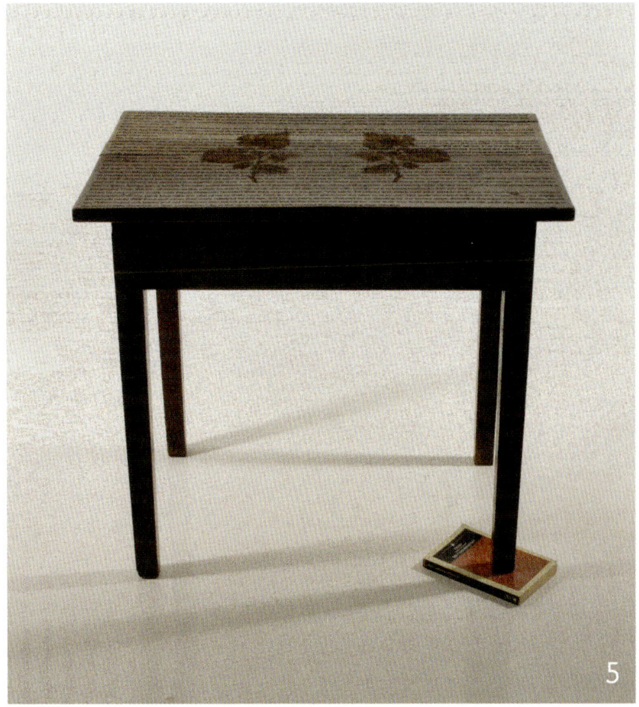

5

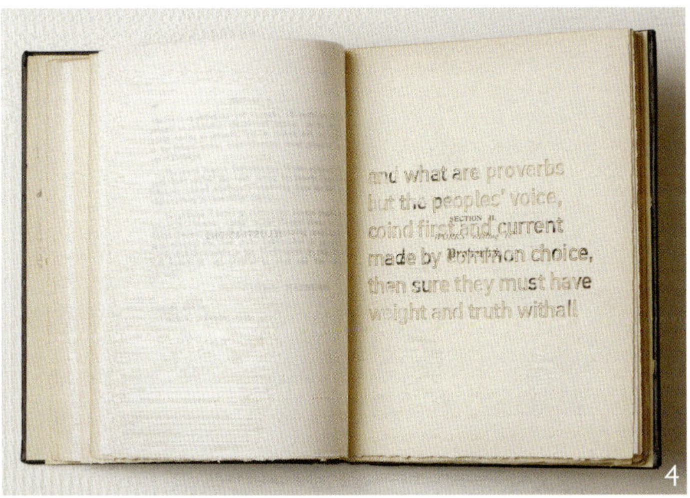

4

Joseph J Field

fieldfinearts@btinternet.com
www.fieldfinearts.co.uk

Joseph J Field (Jo) studied art as a second profession post retirement as a local authority chief officer. He has an HND in Fine Art and MA in Printmaking. He was introduced to artists' books by Guy Begbie, one of his tutors at Hereford.

Writing has always given Jo much pleasure – from professional papers to the short poems around which many of his books are created. Jo takes his inspiration from the world around him. Some of his books record memories of friends and neighbours, others reflect his interest in theology; "love" is a constant theme.

The text of the books is usually archival inkjet but most of the books incorporate some original printing including lino cut, polyester plate lithography, rubber stamps and offset. Jo has exhibited his books and prints widely in Europe but also in the USA.

1
Love
5 x 4.5 cm
Surrey cartridge, cloth covered card covers with rubber stamp motif, slip case.

2
Old Wine
11 x 11 cm
Cloth-covered card, Japanese algae paper, tracing paper, folded and stitched, archival inkjet

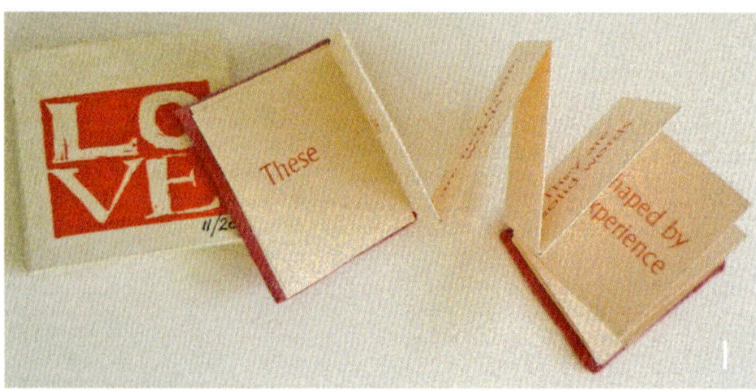

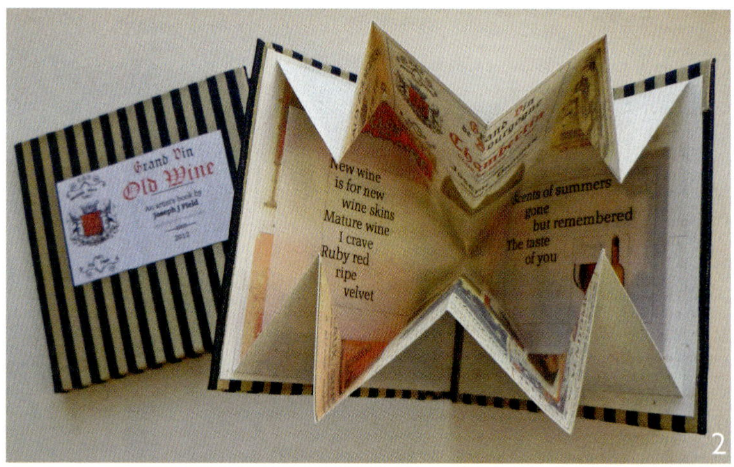

3
Joy to the world
7.5 x 10 cm
Academia paper cover, Japanese Simili paper, polyester plate lithography and archival inkjet

4
Empty Chair
6 x 10 cm
Cloth-covered card, Japanese Simili paper, archival inkjet, rubber stamps, slip case

5
Old McDonald .....
6.5 x 8 cm
Cloth-covered card, Japanese Simili paper, archival inkjet, linocut, slip case

6
Agape
Triangular 5 cm sides
Card, Japanese Simili paper, archival inkjet, rubber stamp

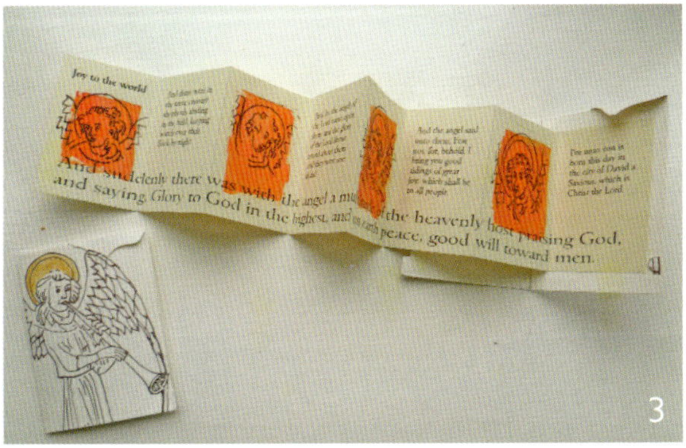

3

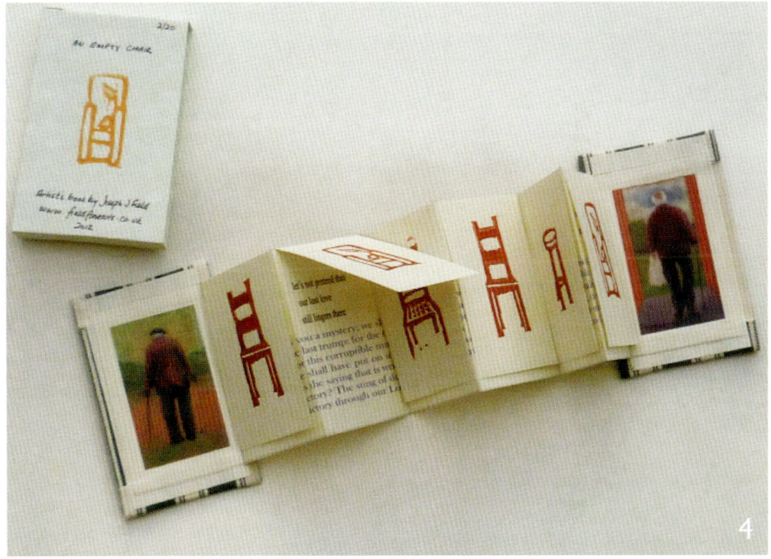
4

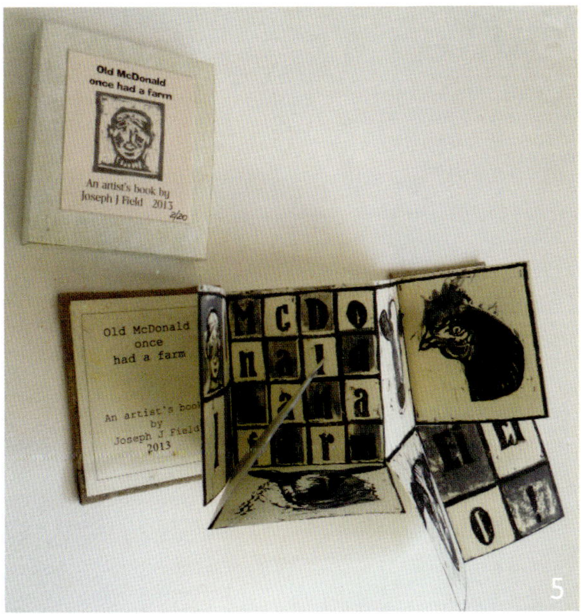

5

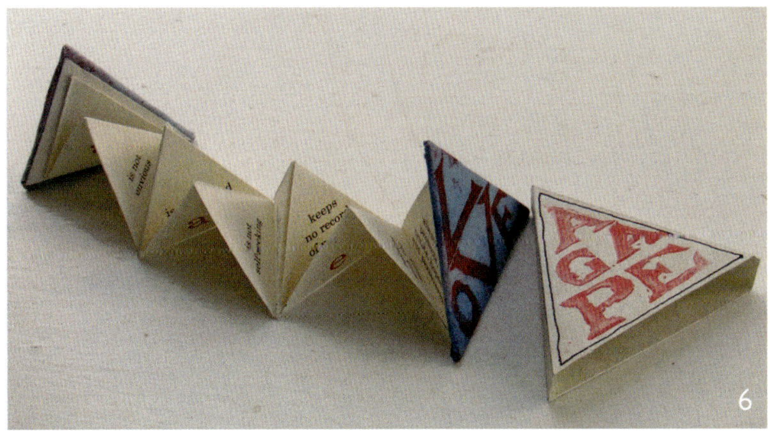

6

Joanna Gibbs
Rag-&-Bone Shop Books

j.gibbs577@btinternet.com
www.artistsbooksonline.com

Joanna Gibbs learnt to bind books at school. Her love of the handmade book was reawakened while studying early modern texts as a visiting lecturer in Renaissance Literature at Goldsmiths In 2007 she set up her small press imprint, Rag-&-Bone Shop Books.

Typically, Joanna writes, illustrates and binds one original artist's book, which she then scans, embellishes and hand binds into a limited edition of ten to 15 books. Joanna often works from digital photographs into which she stitches, overprints with etching, linocut, collage, a manual typewriter, letterpress, and rubber stamps - frequently employing experimental materials, such as baking paper and dress makers' mending fabrics, to further evoke the tactile qualities of the book as object.

Joanna's books are held in private and public collections, including St Bride Library, University College London and the University of Westminster.

1 & 2
Incarcerated Shes
21.5 x 15.5 cm
Inkjet, Bockingford paper, digital photography, linocut, etching, textile covers, open-work spine

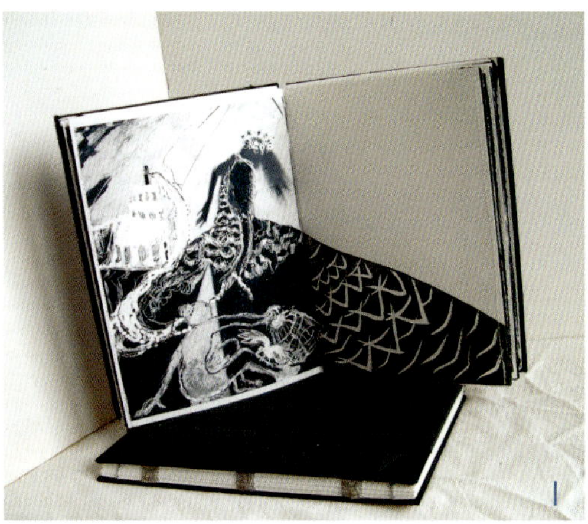

1

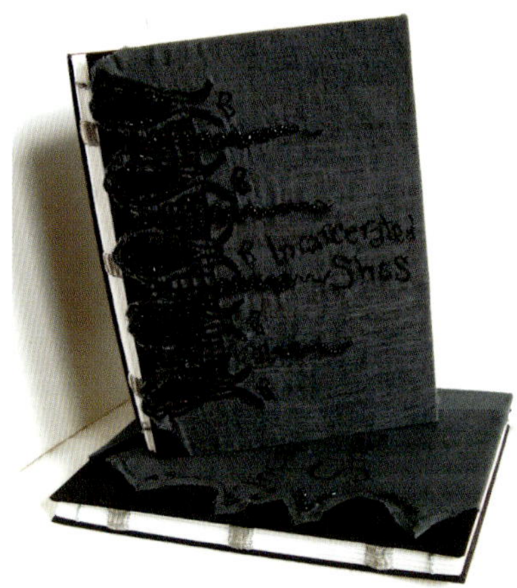

2

3 & 5
Leaf Watermarks
21 x 17 cm
Inkjet, baking paper, chiffon, sewing, digital photography, rubber stamps, open-work spine

4 & 6
By Christ! The Baby Angels
32 x 22 cm
Inkjet, Bockingford paper, digital photography, drypoint, manual typewriter

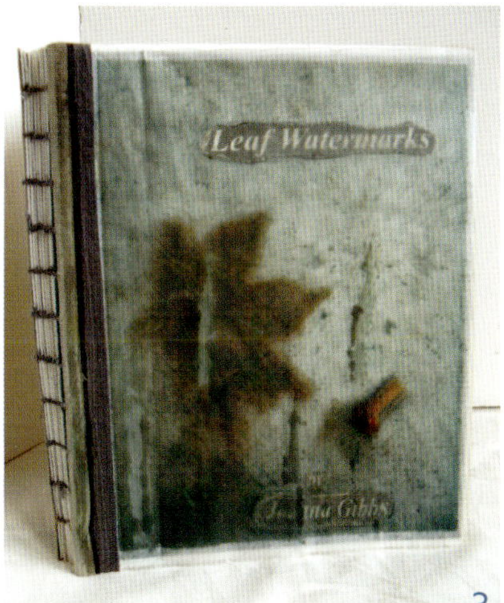

3

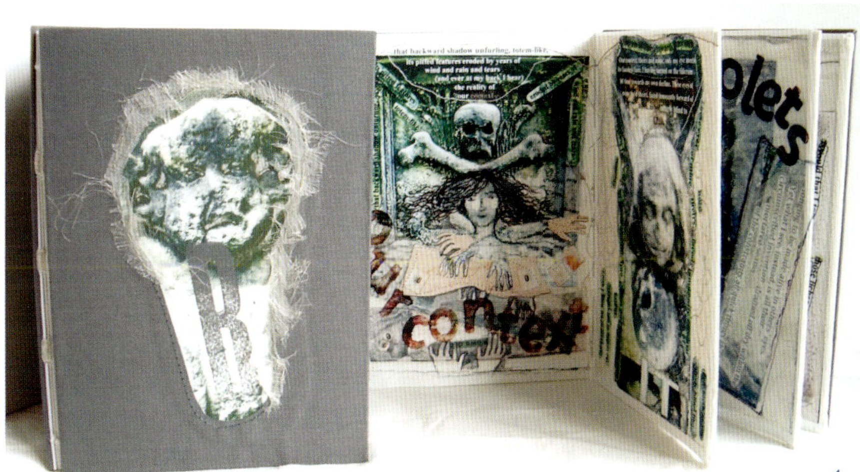

4

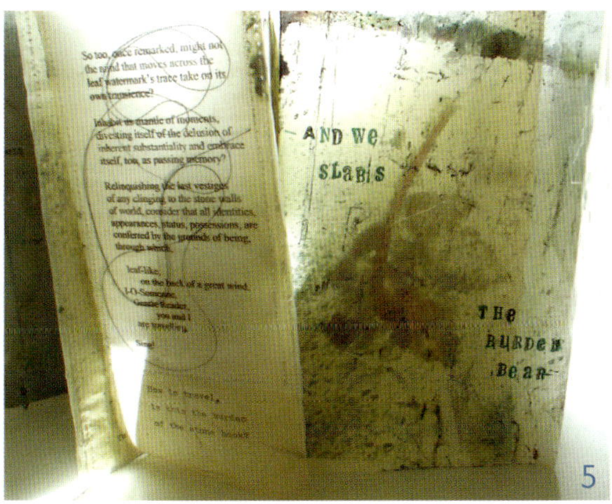

5

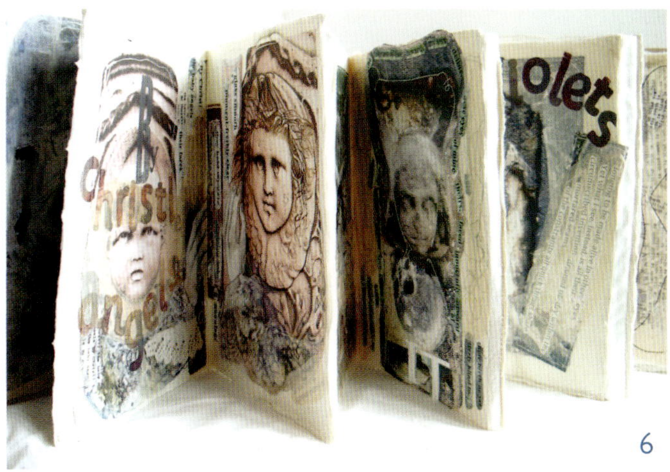

6

Noreen Grant

dusters@mac.com

Noreen Grant is a printmaker and painter living in Suffolk. As a print-maker she works with antique textile and garment-related imagery. Wishing to diversify from making prints viewed only on a wall she has revived an earlier interest in the making of books - held in the hand they are tactile and immediate.

She has used the hinged-accordion binding style to combine mono and intaglio prints of precise patterns, costume pieces and textile fragments. She has printed them in a range of white, silver and black inks. The binding style allows images to be seen in pairs or their entirety when fully open.

Each book in the series is bound in black buckram or bookcloth and contained in a Japanese style four-fold box lined with handmade paper. Her work has been exhibited internationally and is held in public and private collections.

1 & 2

Fragments and Spectres

8.3 x 8.7/8.3 x 53 cm

Intaglio, monoprint and photocopy on Somerset, Sekishu Shi, tracing and handmade paper; board and buckram

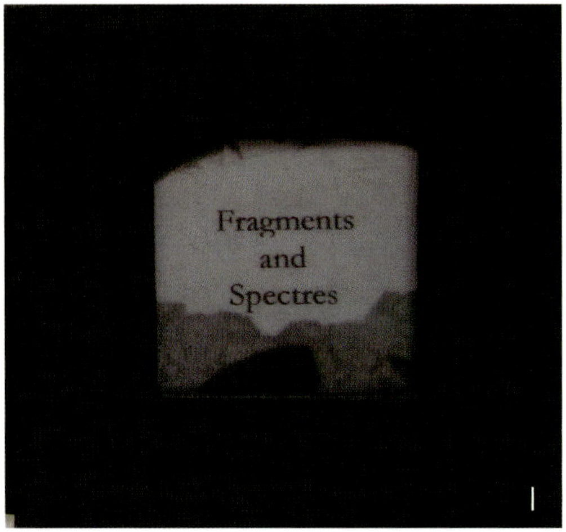

1

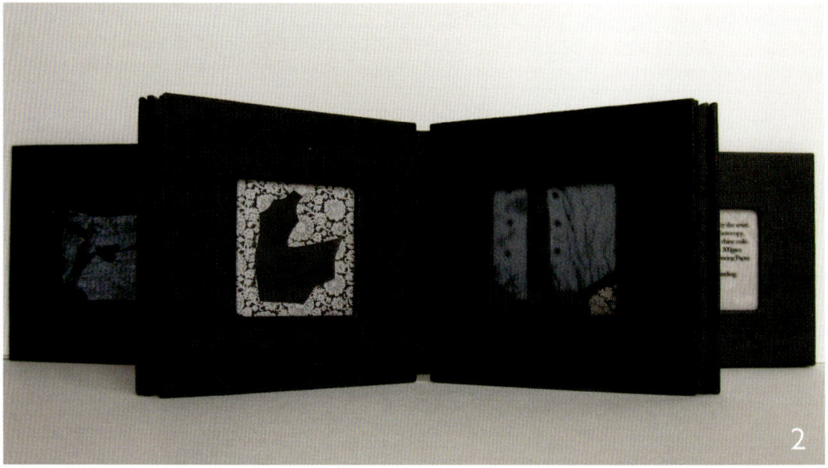

2

Nina Gronw-Lewis

nina@ninaart.co.uk
www.NinaArt.co.uk

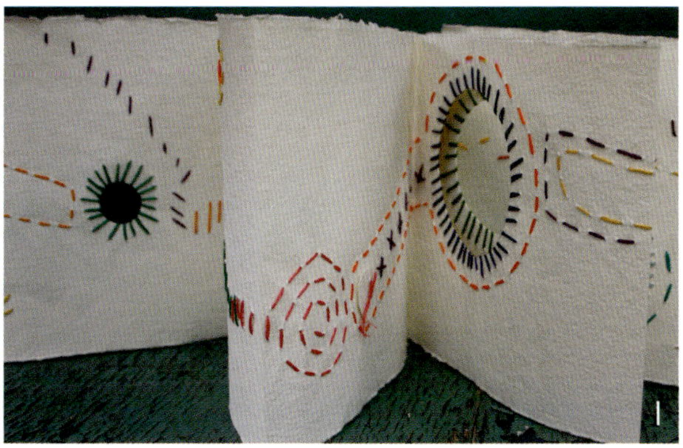

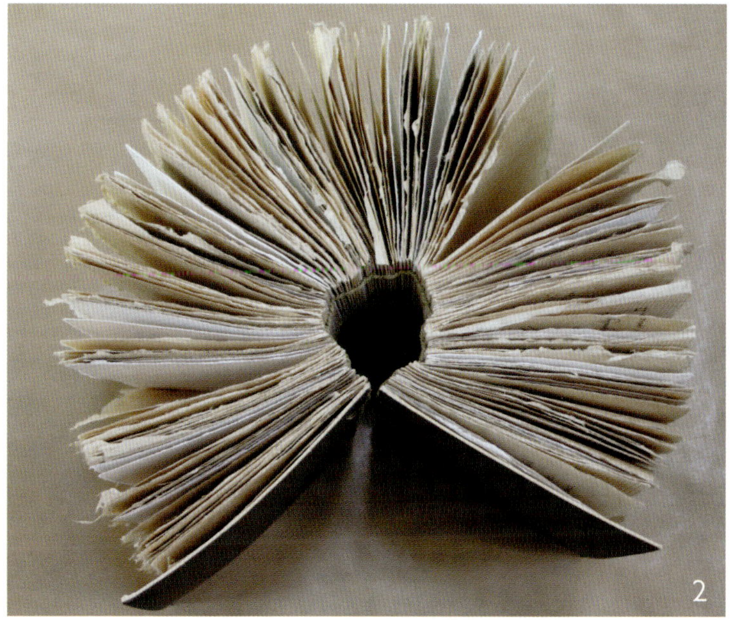

1
Stitch in time
15 x 150 cm
Khadi paper, embroidery thread.

2
'around the world in 180 pages'
h22 x w16 x d16 cm
Handmade papers and coptic binding

3
All together now
10 x 120 cm
Khadi paper, etching ink, gold leaf.

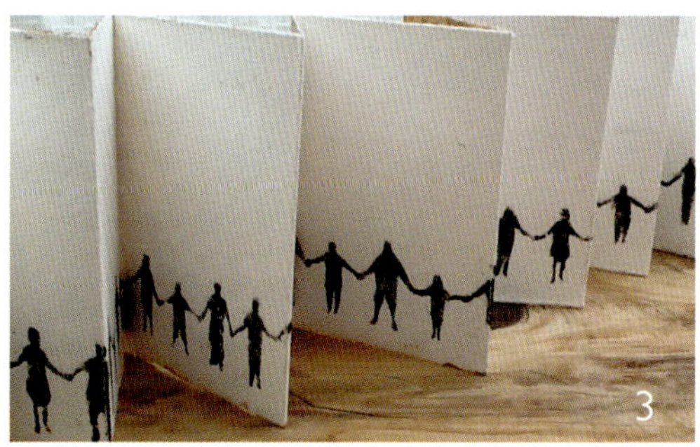

Kitty Guthrie Oakley

seaside.kitty@gmail.com
www.kittyguthrieoakley.com

Kitty Guthrie Oakley is an illustrator who makes books for the fun of it. Combining drawing and handwritten text with simple structures, Kitty creates humorous books that are often inspired by magazines, films and romantic novels from her teen years in the 1960s.

1
Bikini Line
6 x 8 cm, hand drawn and cut out, concertina fold, ink on 220gsm paper

2
Always know when a girl wants kissing
11 x 15 cm, digital prints, card, hand folded and stitched

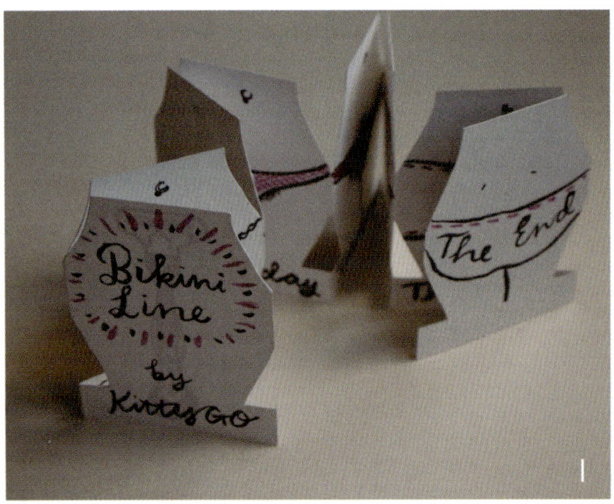

1

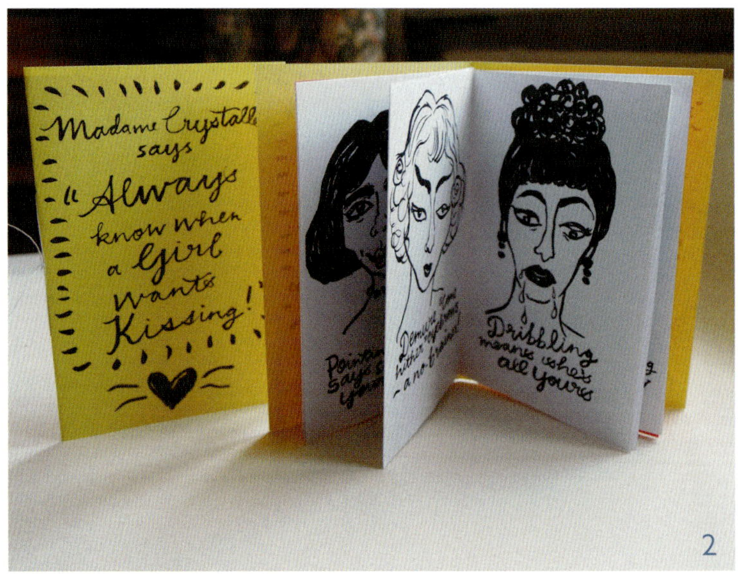

2

Bob Guy

bob.guy264@gmail.com
T: 441691 648862

Bob Guy is a practising printmaker and book artist living in the Welsh hills. His recent practice has been in collaboration with poets, as illustrator/ interpreter of text.

While primarily a traditional printmaker producing wood engravings on a 19th Atlas press, some projects have called for the use of contemporary media, e.g Indigo, a poem by Childe Roland: a boxed set consisting of giclee printed text, folded concertina-wise, embossed covers, a DVD of performance, with percussion soundscape by Rick Wilson.

Current project is a series of wood engravings and hand cut text illustrating the poem "Siwrnai Bob"/"Bob's Journey" by Robin O. Hughes, a distinguished Welsh "bard" (and neighbour). The poem was commissioned to mark the artist's 40 year residency in Montgomeryshire. Bob Guy exhibits with the Society of Wood Engravers and is a member of the www.artistsbooksonline.com collective.

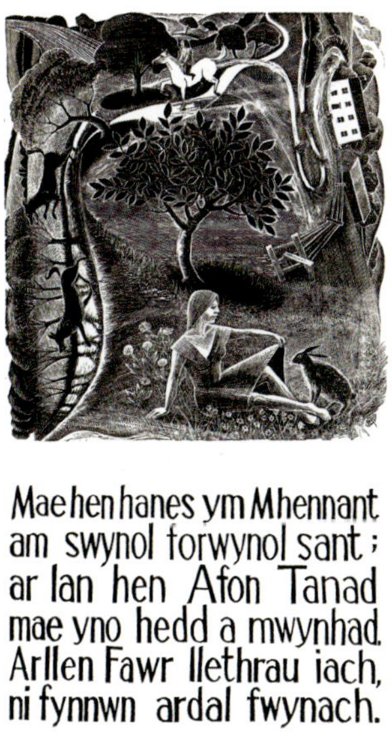

1

1 A legend of Pennant
33 x 25 cm
Wood engraving with hand cut text

2 The Vision of Indigo Jones
Box size 12.5 cm sq.
Dyed & embossed rag covers to concertina style digital prints;
DVD of performance

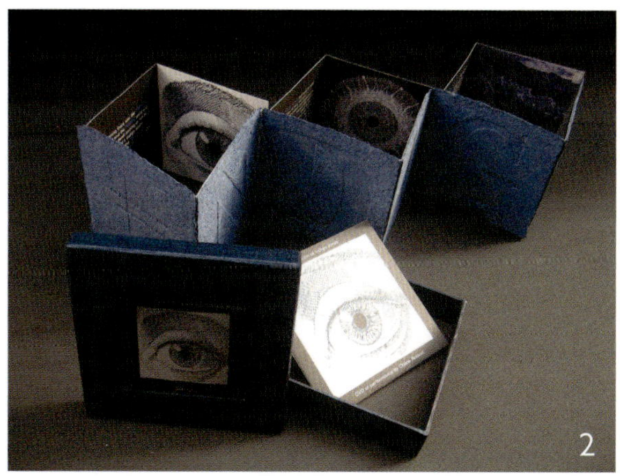
2

Hestan Isle Press

Barntimpin House
St. Anns, Lockerbie DG11 1HL
hestanislepress@btinternet.com
www.hestanislepress.co.uk
T: 0156 470222

1 The Holy Spirit – Lady of the Doves
2 How is it with you in the shape of a…?
3 The Seafarer

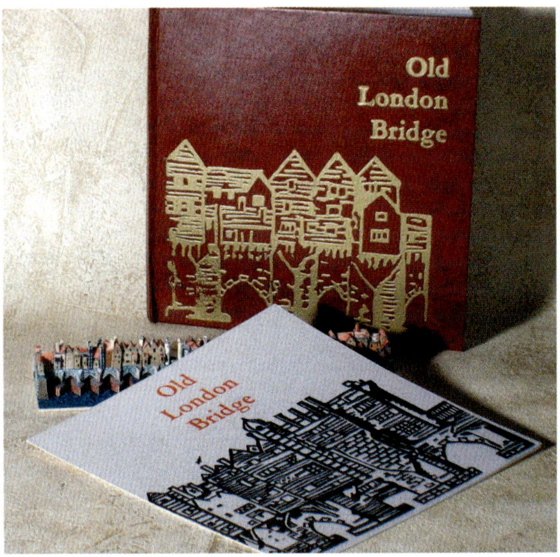

Peter and Frances Grant at the Hestan Isle Press, make Rather Special Books. They are printed on the Hand-press from individual letters of metal type, and all are signed limited editions. Some are miniature Books, some larger, some are illustrated by Frances Grant (who also designs the slip-cases), and all are hand-bound using artificial leathers, book-cloths, and interesting papers. Books Worth Keeping!

The books are bought by collectors all over Britain, America and Canada, and some can be found in the Edward Clark Rare Book Collection at Edinburgh's Napier University, the University of Virginia Library, and the Victoria and Albert Museum Library, London.

They can also be seen regularly at Craft and Book Fairs – such as the Glasgow International Artists' Book Fair, and the Edinburgh Artists Book-mart.

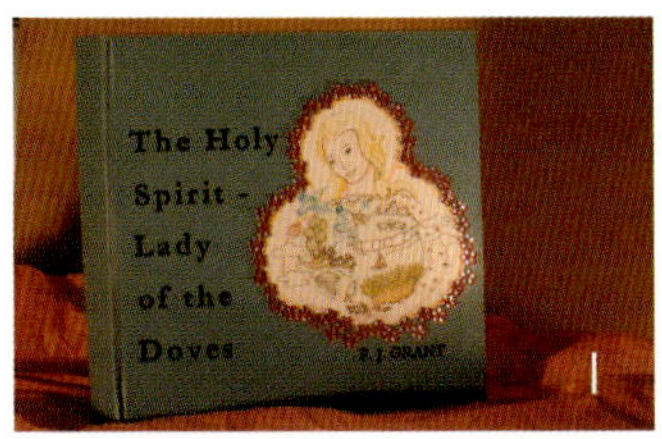

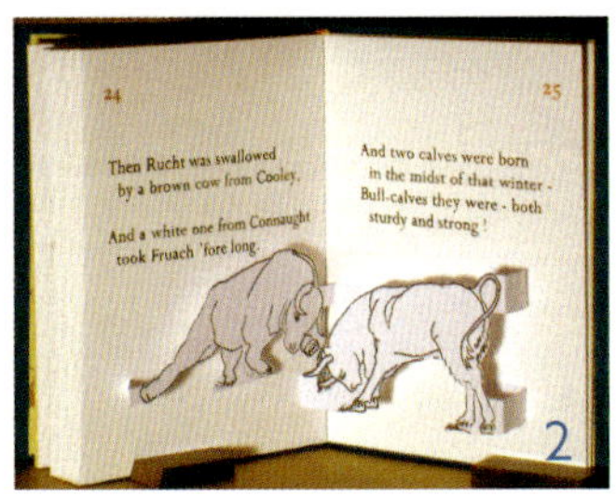

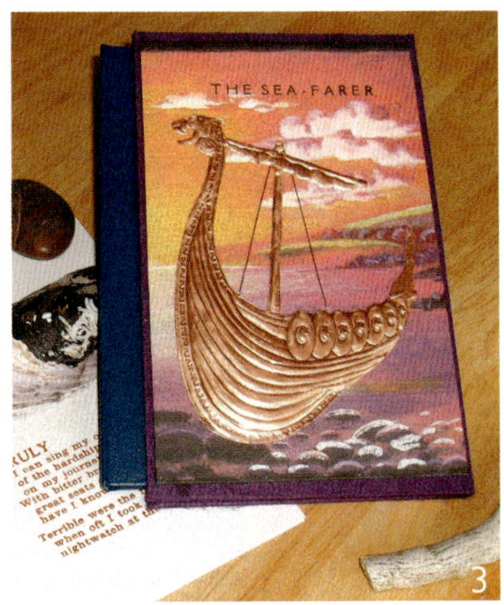

ABCD (cont'd)

ABCD at Dove Studios
cm@craftgalleries.co.uk
Also see pages 9, 33 & 37

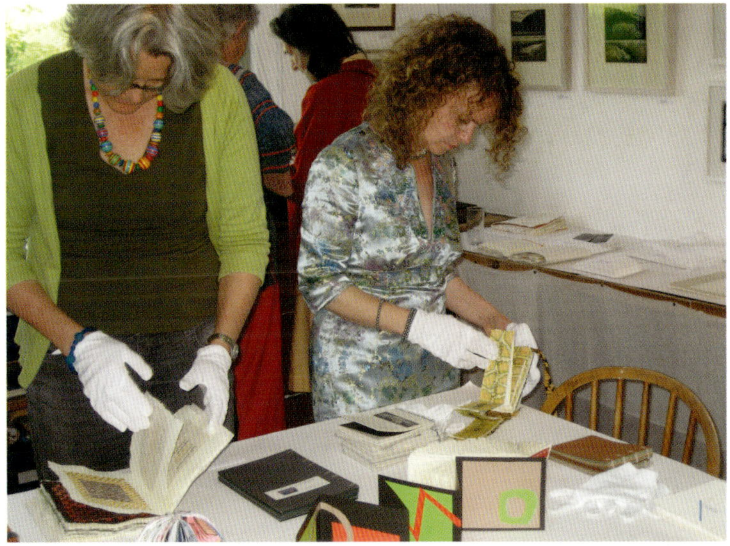

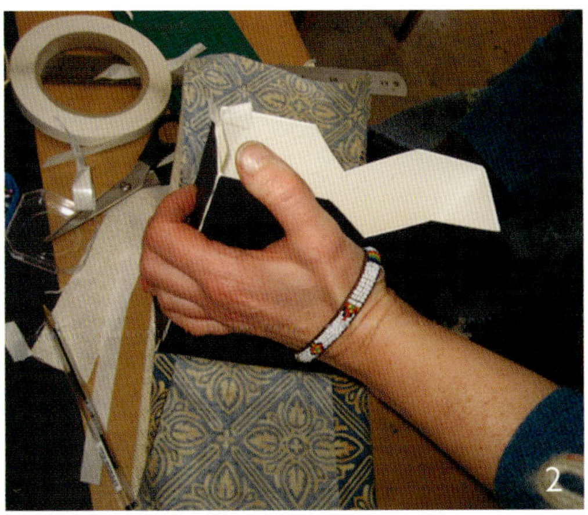

1 Exhibition of books at Dove Studios

2 Thalia Brown at work

3 Found *by Karen Young*

4 Ways to Reach the Open Boat *16 x 21 cm edition of 200 by Ama Bolton*

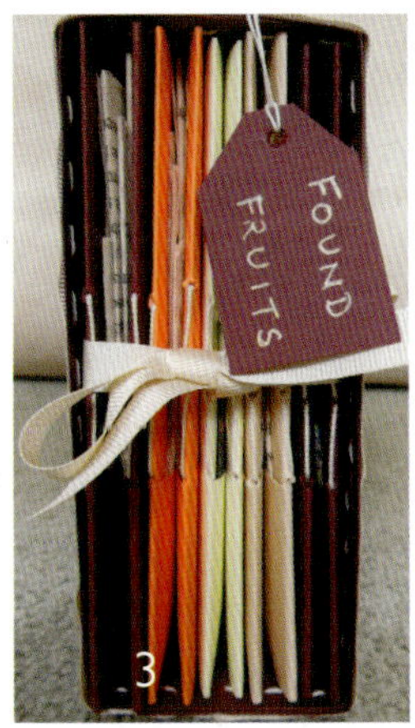

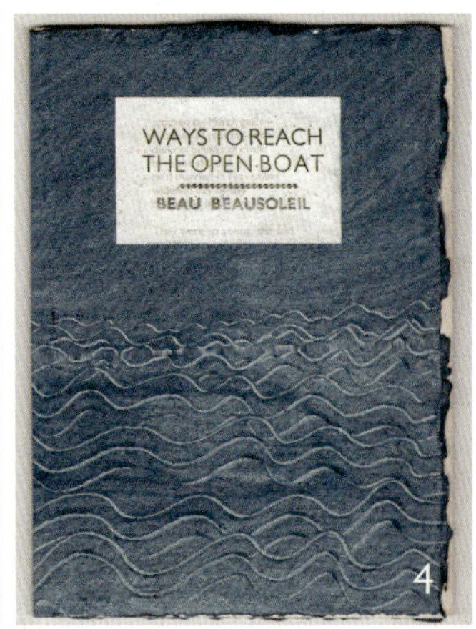

Andrea Hill

andrea.hill@btinternet.com

1

Silence that Sang
25.5 x 16 cm
Silk needle box, pages collaged with text and sepia photographs

2

Candles & Shadows
14 x 21.5 cm
Altered book bound in scrim and wax with gold ink

Andrea Hill has been making altered artists' books since she graduated from Goldsmiths in 1989.
Her work deals with memory and loss, she uses found objects and old photographs, text is torn or cut from found hardback books by obscure authors, the title often being of importance, to make her own text.

Silk, scrim, plaster of paris and wax are often used, symbolic materials i.e plaster of paris to bind wounds, wax to seal old letters. Andrea exhibits her books at various artists book fairs, galleries and Libraries in the UK and abroad.

Her work is also found in artists book collections in the UK and Italy, and various publications regarding artists books.

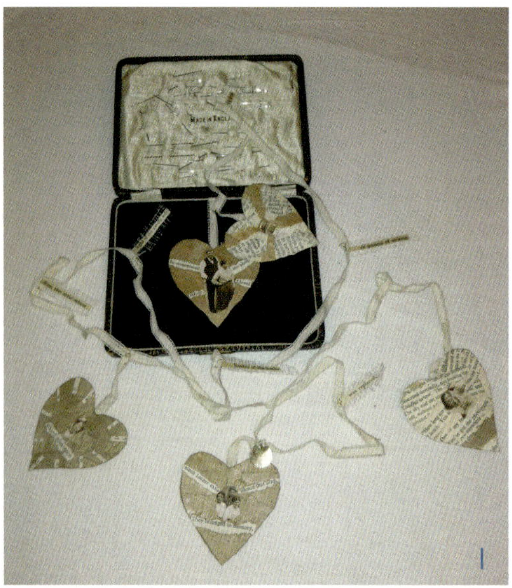

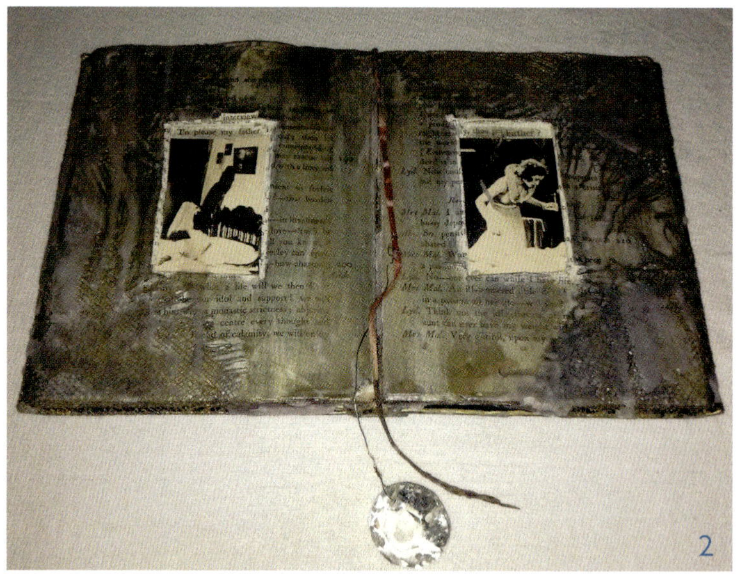

Pat Hodson

pat@pathodson.co.uk
www.pathodson.co.uk

Pat Hodson exploits the essential sensuality of having to open, unfold, turn the page of a book. Pages are layered, tactile; enclosed in boxes of waxed, burnished collage. With colour over colour and complex interweaving of image with word; glimpses of fundamental patterns, hidden myth, lost paths and forgotten journeys.

1
Red through Red
(box detail)
Encaustic collage – waxed fused layers of paper, silk, thread and acrylic

2
Red through Red
19.5 × 235 cm extended
Abaca tissue, silk, recycled fragments, crayon, wax. Epson pigmented inks

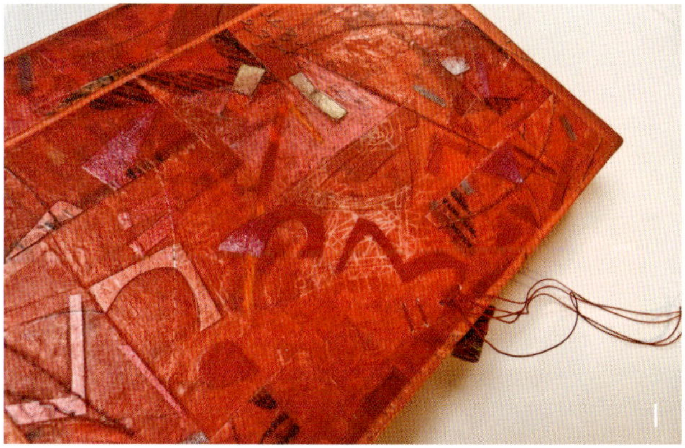
1

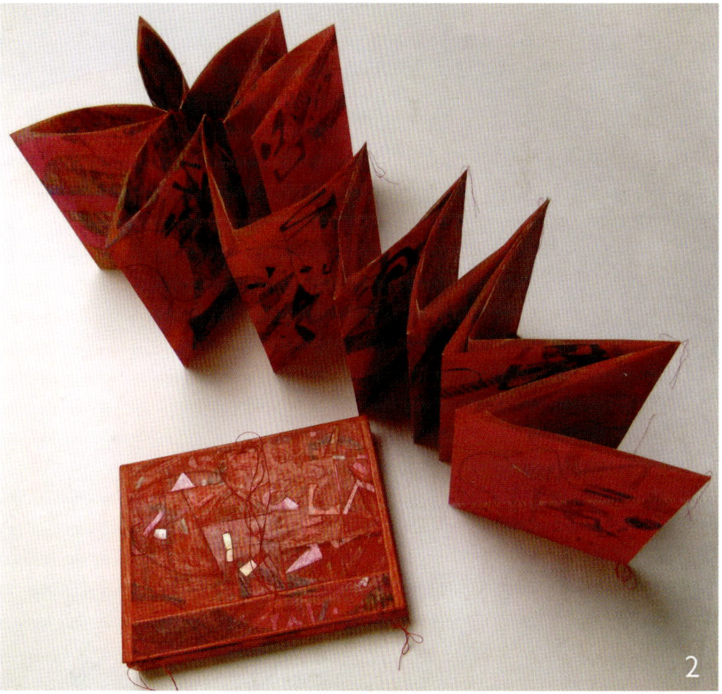
2

David Howe

davidhow961@ aol.co.uk

Much of my work is engaged with the nature of rivers, concentrating on the estuary of the river Stour in Suffolk. My aim is to produce a visual response to the estuary that allows the creative expression of information I have gathered. The information includes lists of bird and fish types that inhabit the estuary, as well as emotional responses gathered on visits to the area. I also use objects found on walks along local streams and rivers in conjunction with handwriting to represent creatures living in the water and to articulate a sense of flow.

My most recent work uses handwritten words to communicate the frequency of local wildlife. The text is written on gathered wood and is recorded daily, then arranged in the form of a diary where one branch represents one day of recordings.

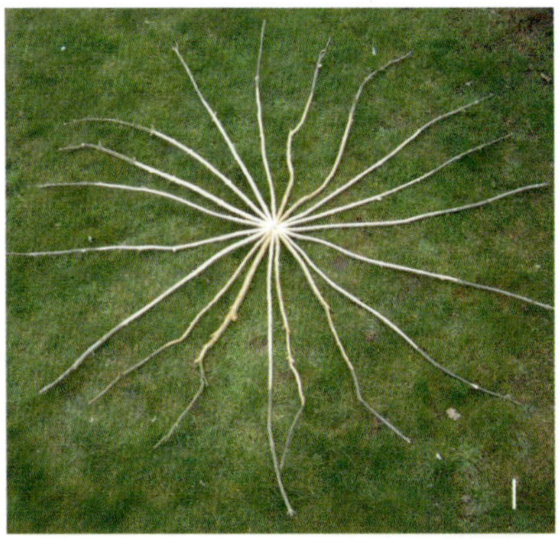

1

1, 2 & 3

Diary & details
250 x 250 cm
Hand written text on branches cut from the hedgerow.

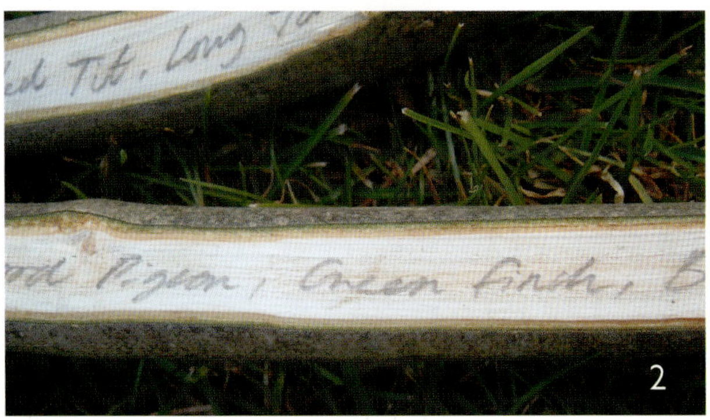

2

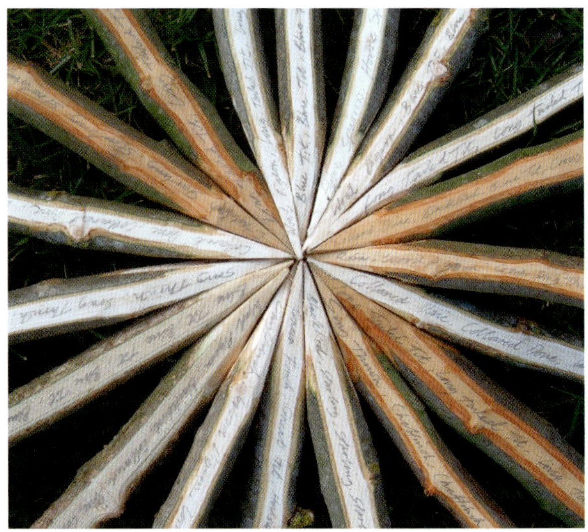

3

4 & 5
Estuary & detail
120 x 28 cm
Hand written text on Snowden Paper held between sheets of glass.

6
River
150 x 10 cm
Hand written text on wood found by the river.

7
Leaf
22 x 30 cm
Found leaf with hand written text on Snowden paper.

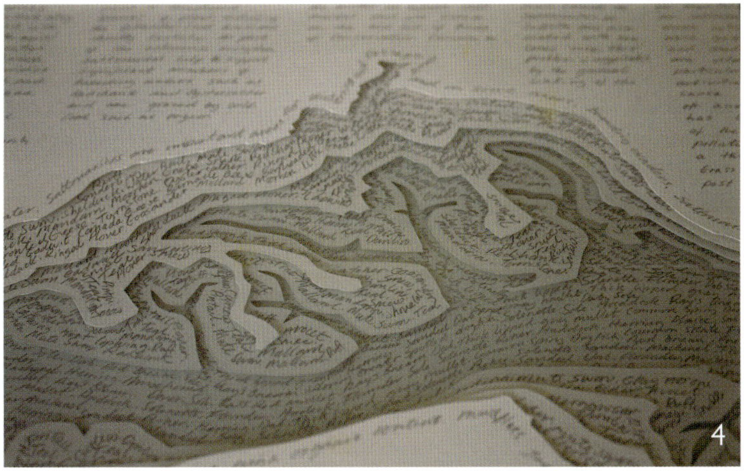
4

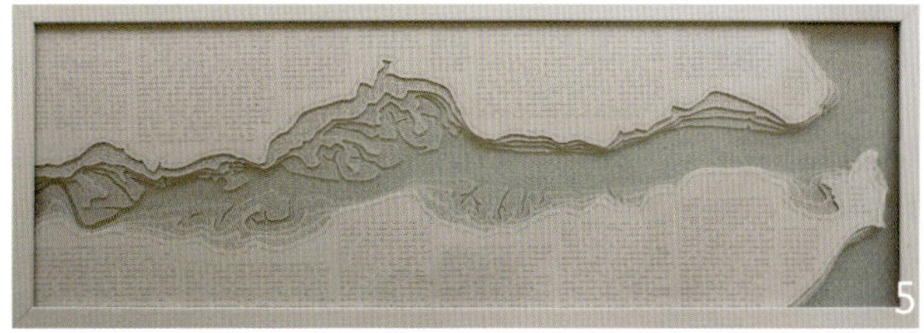
5

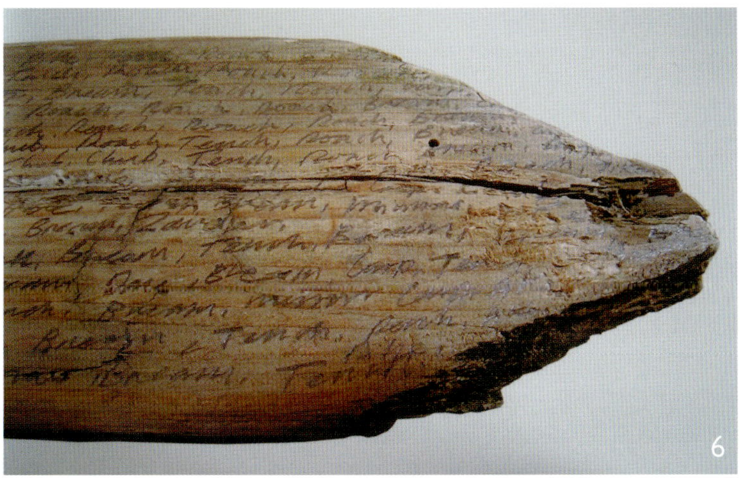
6

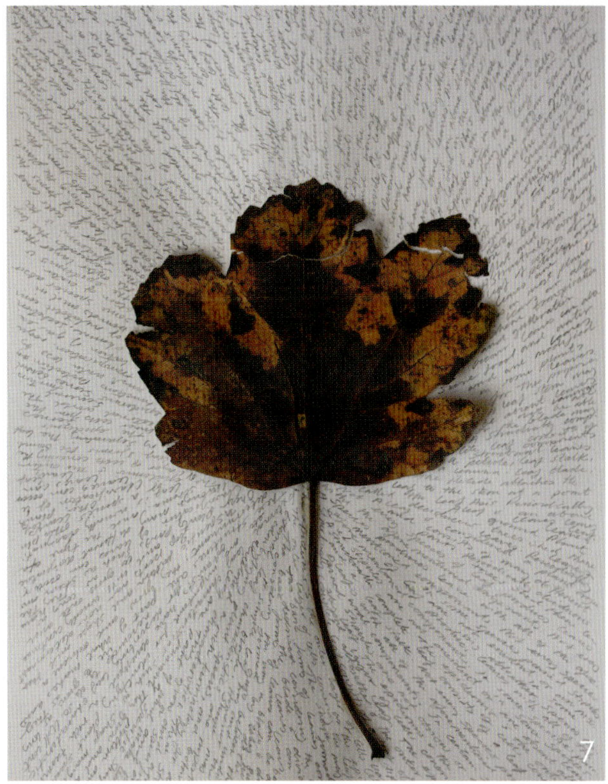
7

Heather Hunter Books

heather@hunterbooks.co.uk
www.hunterbooks.co.uk

In her Artists' books she writes all her own text, produces her own images and constructs her own bindings.

The 3 dimensional book structures that constantly provide visual and tactile surprises make her books. She has been making artists' books since 1993 but recently has ventured into altered books. Research introduced her to writers that have had conversations with the text of another. Her altered books reflect this philosophy.

She graduated from Oxford Brookes University with a BSc. Hons in Psychology and Visual Studies. Her books are in private collections and in University libraries. Winner of the Brigit Skiöld Memorial Trust Artist's Book Purchase Award at London Artists Book Fair for Observer Series – Music.

She is at present Artist - in - Residence at Turn End Garden, Haddenham. www.turnend.org.uk.

1
Detail from 2
Word pool cut, exposed for the found poems in the second book.

2
Observer Series- Garden Flowers
19.5 x 9.5 x 18 cm Discarded book., second book case bound. Poems and images digital

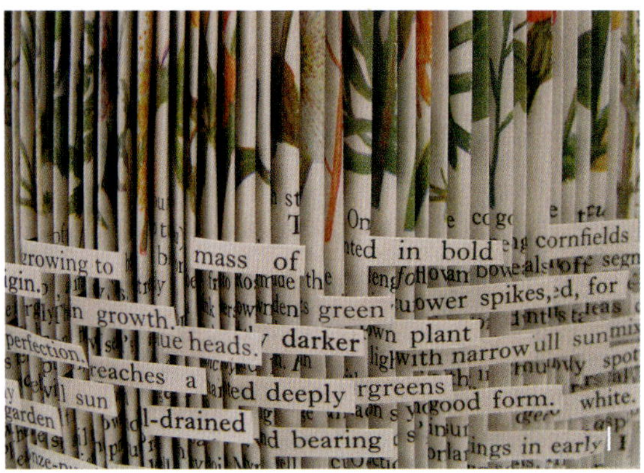

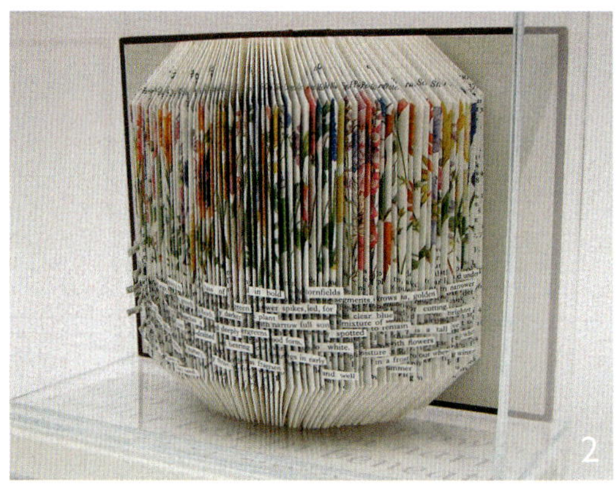

3
Yes
12 x 16.5 x 2 cm
Card, paper, gelatin printing with added stencils and hand - written text.

4
Famous Proba - Found
20 x 20 x 2.5 cm
Card, hand printed and digital papers. 'Woven and interlocking book structures' binding.

5
Yes
12 x 16.5 x 2 cm
Card, paper, envelopes. Hand printed board book.

6
Snowdrop
11 cm triangular
Card, digital images on paper. Wire edged bound Lygia Clark inspired

7
Detail of 4
Verse of found poem taken from Boccaccio's text.

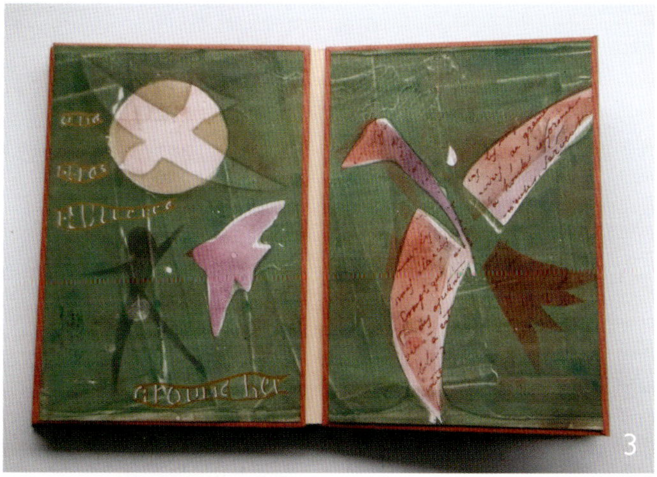
3

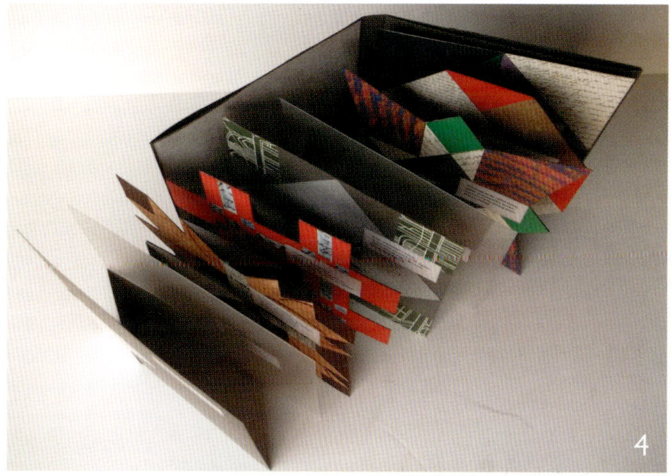
4

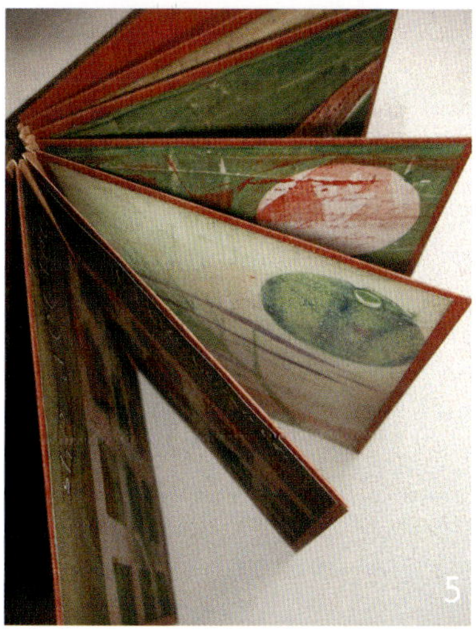
5

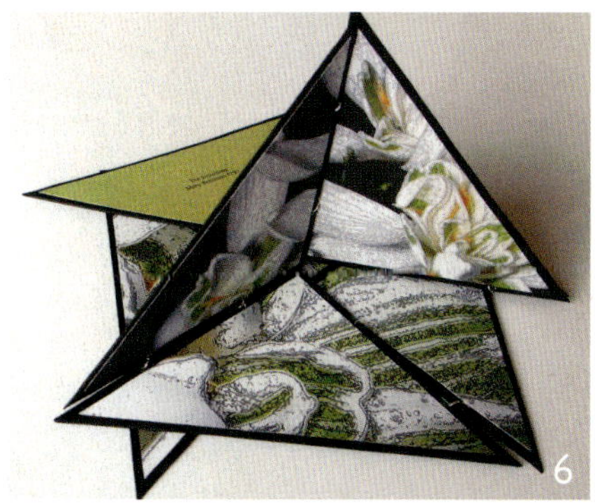
6

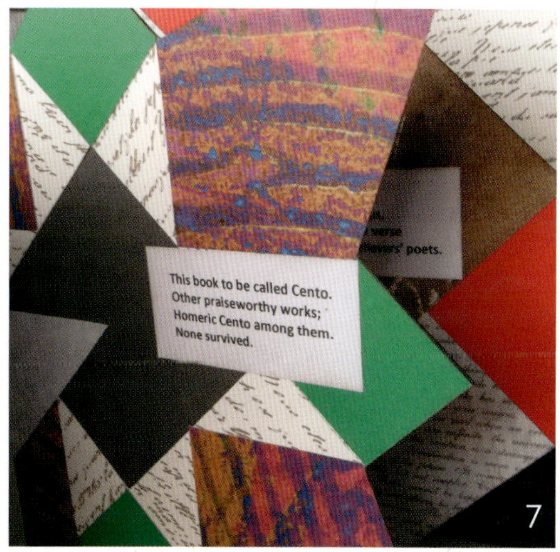

7

Victoria Keeble

victoriakeeble@hotmail.com
www.victoria-keeble.com

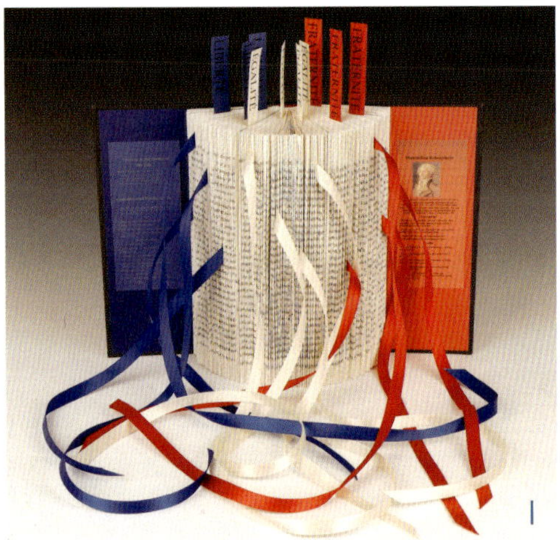

1

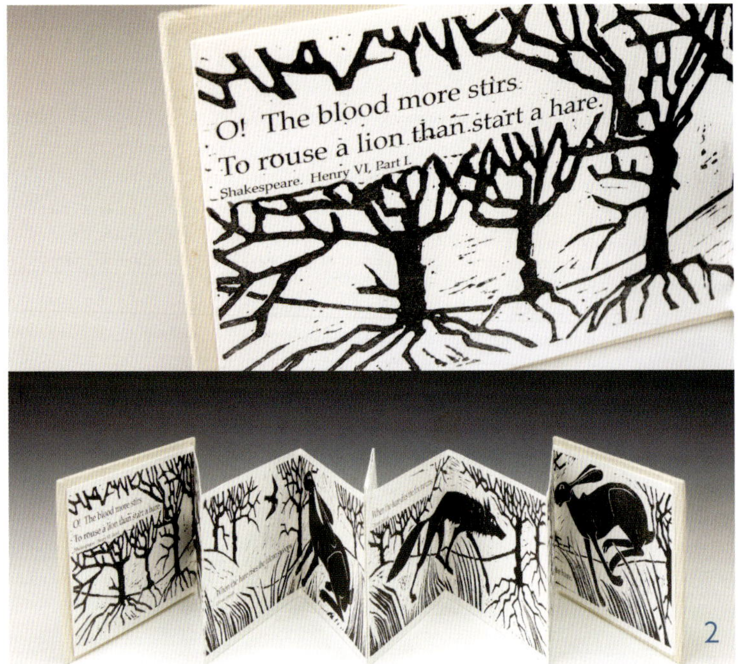

2

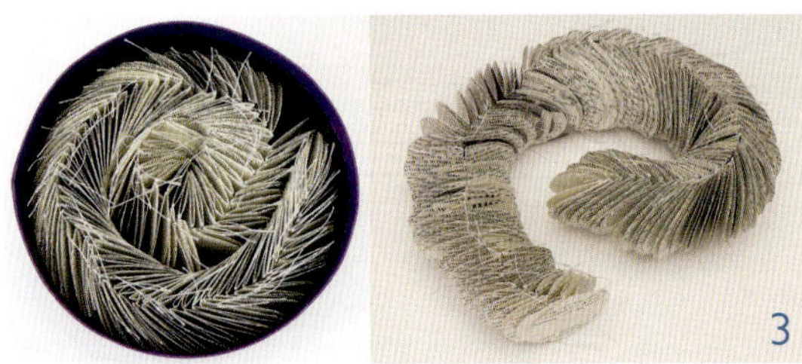

3

1
Tricolore
29 x 19.5 cm
Altered book with inserts and ribbons

2
Hare
16 x 12 cm
Linocut & print on handmade paper, covers: Lokta. Concertina folded

3
Bookworm
41 x 5 cm
Altered book pages cut & sewn onto webbing

Susie Leiper

susieleiper@hotmail.com
www.susieleiper.com
www.theartistbookgroup.org.uk

1
Noctambulism
24.5 x 12.5 cm
Star book: gouache on card. Text from The Wild Places *by Robert Macfarlane*

2
Scene linked to scene
20 x 10 cm
Double-sided concertina in silk covers: mixed media. Text from 'The Prelude' *by William Wordsworth.*

The oriental origin of the concertina book format is often forgotten. As a medium for display, it is unbeatable. Susie Leiper's books incorporate poetry, text, image, often enclosed in covers of silk or wood. Each book is a one off.

Trained as a calligrapher and painter, and with a passion for Chinese art and language, Susie exhibits regularly and has won numerous awards. Her books are in the Royal Collection, the Fitzwilliam Museum, the National Library of Scotland (1) and Edinburgh College of Art. She lives and works in Edinburgh where she is a member of the Artist Book Group led by Jenny Smith.

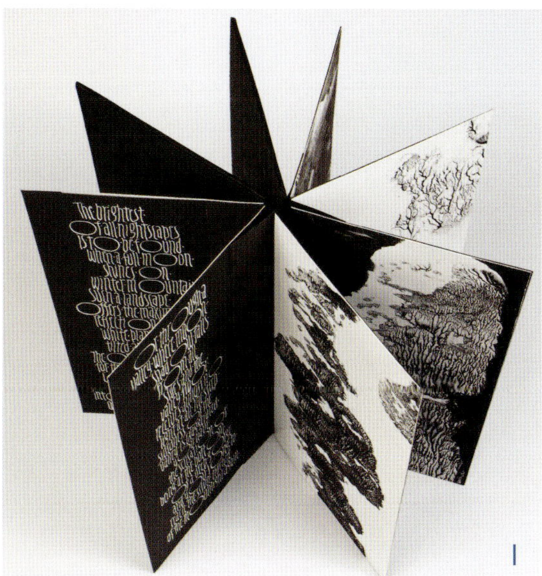

1

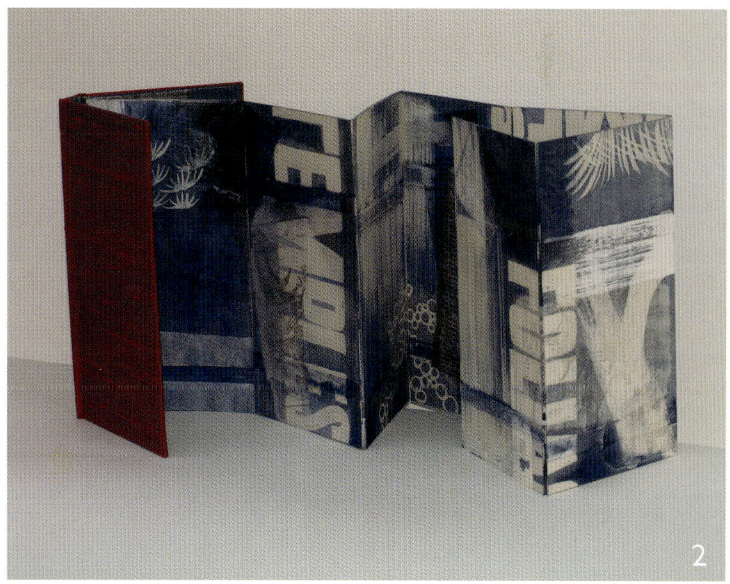

2

Siobhan Martin

mail@paulsiobhan.com
www.siobhanmartin.moonfruit.com

Sound Chimney - One side represents the whirling sound of the wind, the other, the sounds of two collared doves that sat on the chimney and made extraordinary noises.

The sounds came down the chimney into our sitting room. This is my attempt at trying to represent all those noises. I sat and listened to all the sounds and converted them to into recognisable 'words'. Many people, encountering the sound chimney, try to read the words, resulting in a wonderful impromptu sound performance!

Sound Nest - The cut out 'sounds' are those that baby birds make in the nest every spring to the delight of my two cats who then know exactly where to find them! The 'ball' of sound is hand cut from paper, each band is slightly smaller than the last which means that they fit together albeit loosely. The nest is always different each time assembled.

1
Sound Chimney
24 cm ht x 16 cm base width Paper.
Hand cut original. Laser cut edition 100.

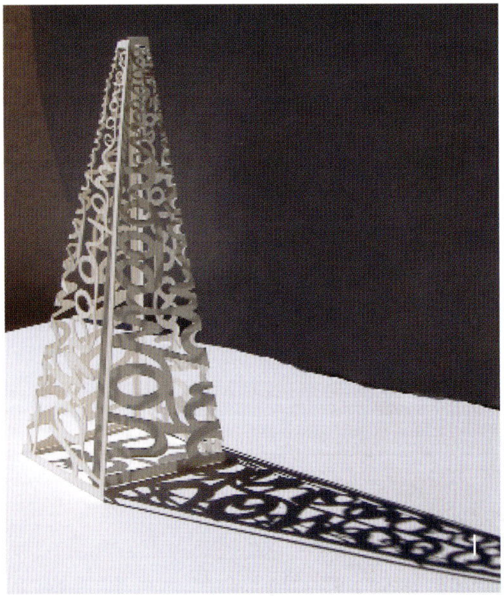

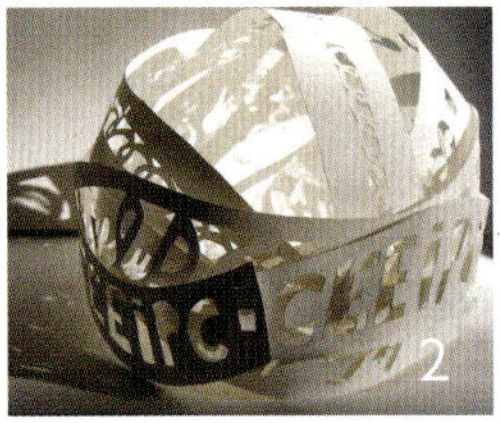

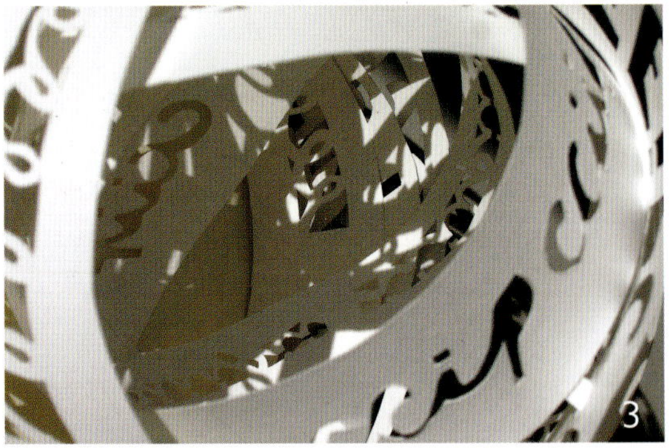

2 & 3
Sound Nest
20cm diam
Hand cut paper

Caroline Mornement

cm@craftgalleries.co.uk
www.bcfbooks.co.uk

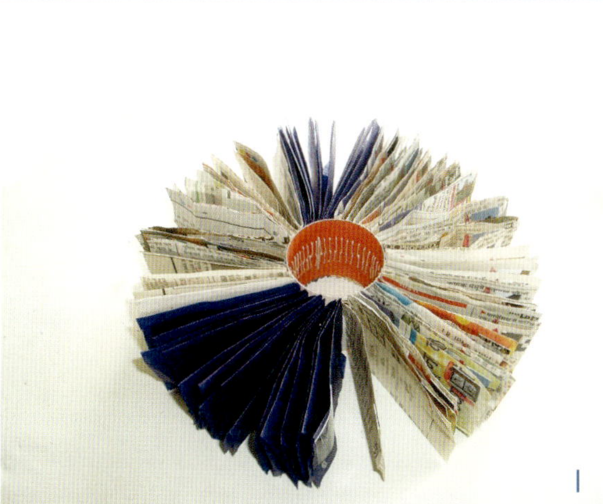

1

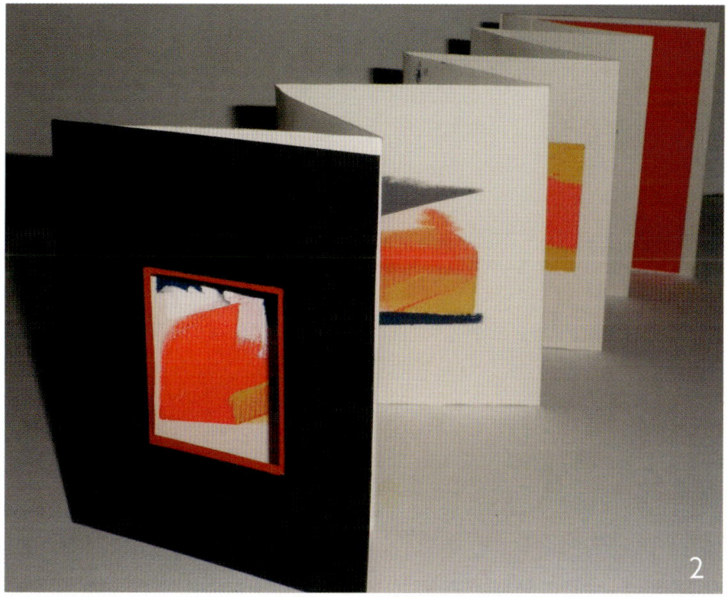

2

1

Around India
6 x 19 cm diam
Indian newspaper, tissue paper & mini digital photos

2

Travels through India
12 x 10 cm closed. Card covered concertina book with screen - printed content on Fabriano paper

3

Hope is .....
7 x 4 x 4 cm
Card box with folded, etched content on Somerset paper

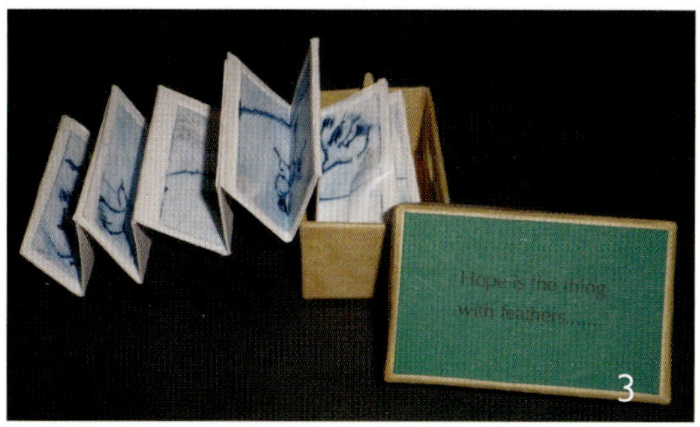

3

Sarah Morpeth

sarah@sarahmorpeth.com
www.sarahmorpeth.com

1
Carsaig 704203
21 x 14 x 75 cm
Paper printed and shredded; sprayed with acrylic ink and hand bound. One off.

2
Catriona's Second Book
55 x 60 x 60 cm
Hand cut paper; gouache paint, bookcloth, wire. One off.

Sarah Morpeth's artist's books take their inspiration from a 1945 film called "I Know Where I'm Going". She returns to this repeatedly, using the script, characters, locations and stories in her work.

In her books she explores the relationship between form and content - the words dictate the shape of the book. She also seeks to express a sense of the importance of the physical presence of a book and the effect that books can have on their readers - that they contain worlds, that they cannot be bounded by their covers. Her pages often spill out and explode from the book; flora and fauna escape their papery cages and take flight. Sarah works to commission and her books are held in a number of public collections, including the Tate Gallery and the Yale Centre for British Art.

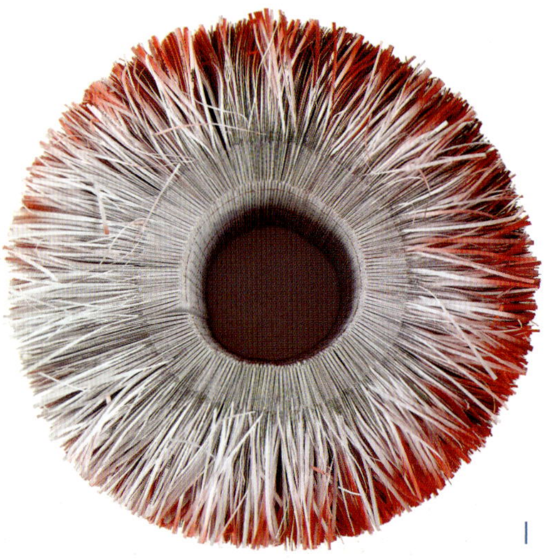

1

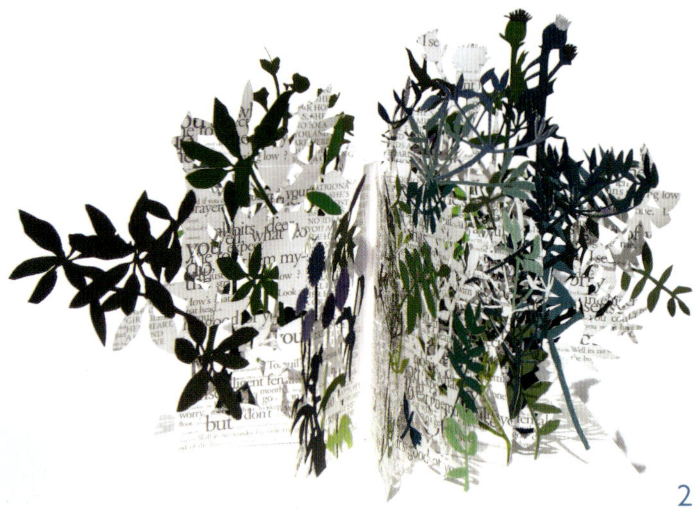

2

3
'To the End'
18 x 18 x 90 cm
Tunnel book with printed paper, bookcloth, concertina sides. One off.

4
Robert's Book
10 x 10 x 200 cm
Concertina book with machine-stitched binding. One off.

5
Catriona's Book
14 x 21 x 2.5 cm
Hand cut paper, hand-bound book. One off.
Photo: Gill Moore

6
The Third Rope
15.5 x 16 x 1 cm when (closed)
Cut paper, concertina sides, hand bound. Edition of 30.

7
'Now, Master Torquil'
2.5. x 12.5 x 1 cm (closed)
Cut paper, bookcloth Edition of 30.

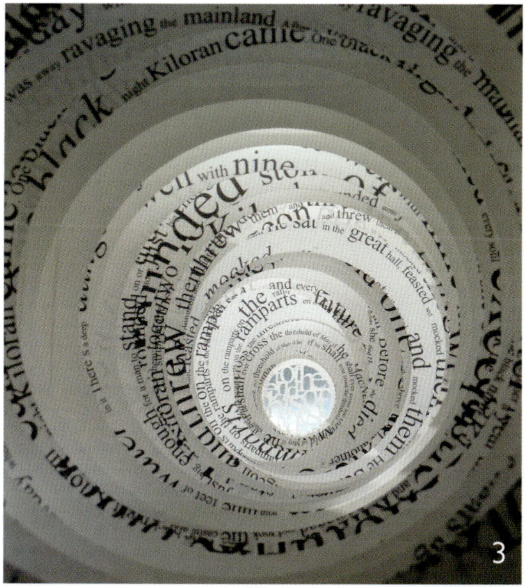

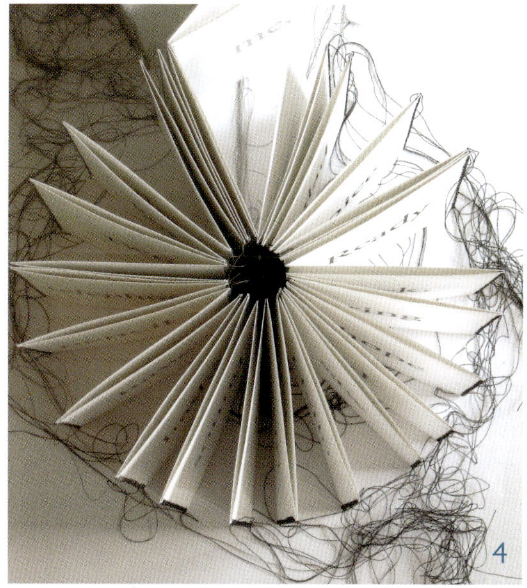

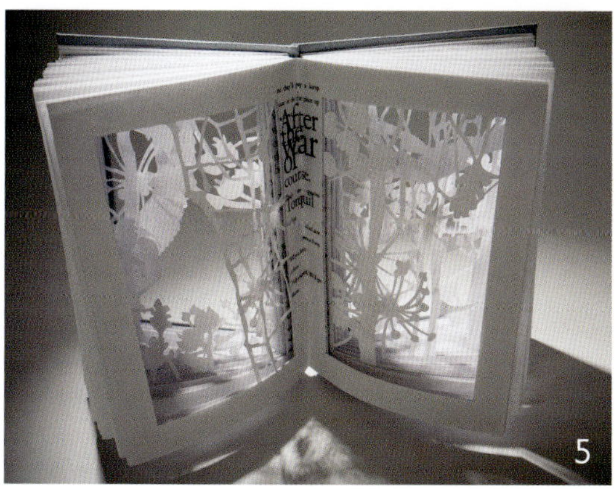

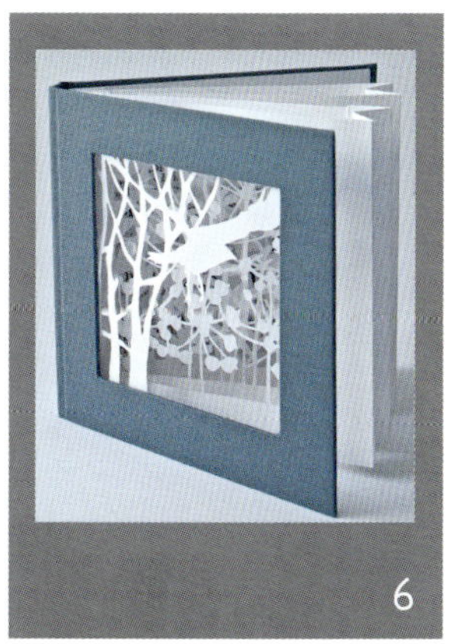

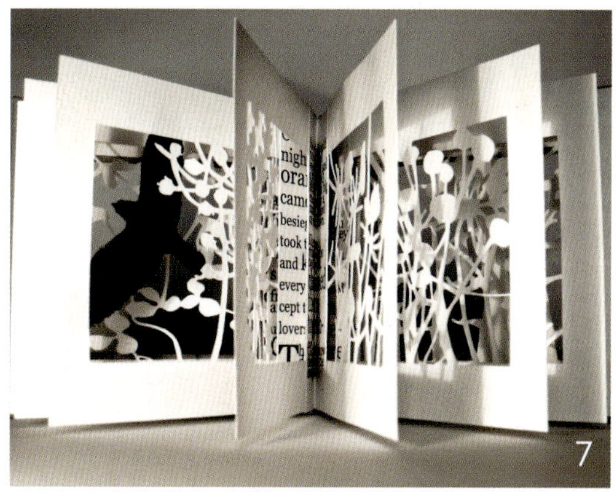

The Old School Press

info@theoldschoolpress.com
www.theoldschoolpress.com

There is little that is predictable about The Old School Press except that it takes pleasure in fine type and paper and a variety of binding styles and materials. Themes are hard to discern but architecture, Italy, and printing history are threads that often return. We like to work with artists who share our fondness for colour and strong line. Our presses are old, but our type is generally cast afresh for each title or hand-set from case; mould-made and hand-made papers predominate. The resulting editions are generally small – perhaps 100 copies – and output is low, anywhere between three and no new titles in a year. We take care and care takes time.

Martyn & Angela Ould

1
Winter Light
43 x 31 cm
Bound in dyed crushed Italian calf with ribbon ties

2
Palladio's Homes
36.5 x 25.5 cm
Linocuts and line drawings printed letterpress

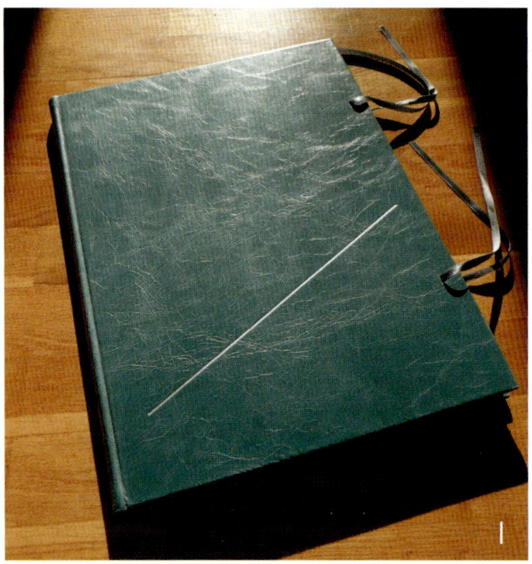

1

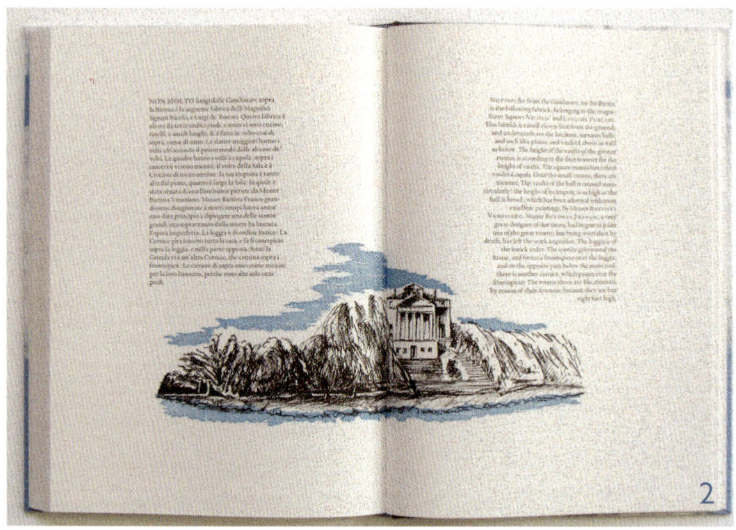

2

3
Henry James Sat Here
28 x 23 cm
Zigzag of letterpress poems and giclée images on Somerset

4
Palladio's Homes
36.5 x 25.5 cm
Letterpress Dante on Amalfi HMP with Cave Paper HMP covers

5
tokonoma
37 x 28 cm
Letterpress Perpetua and woodcuts on Japanese HMP in a display box

6
Venice Visited
27.5 x 20.5 cm
Letterpress Caslon on English HMP with pochoir

7
Winter Light
43 x 31 cm
Letterpress Caslon and giclée on Somerset

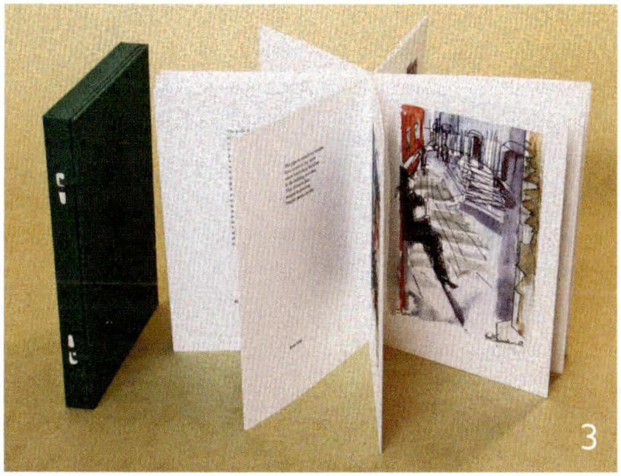
3

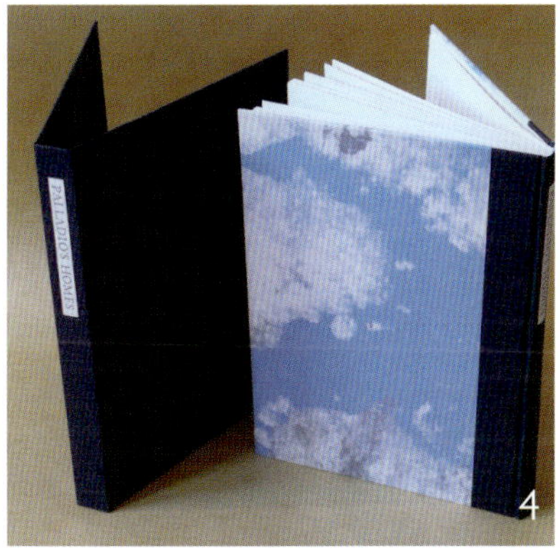

4

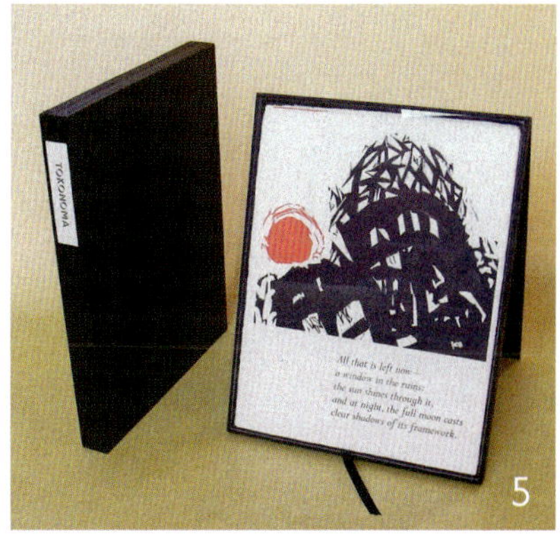

5

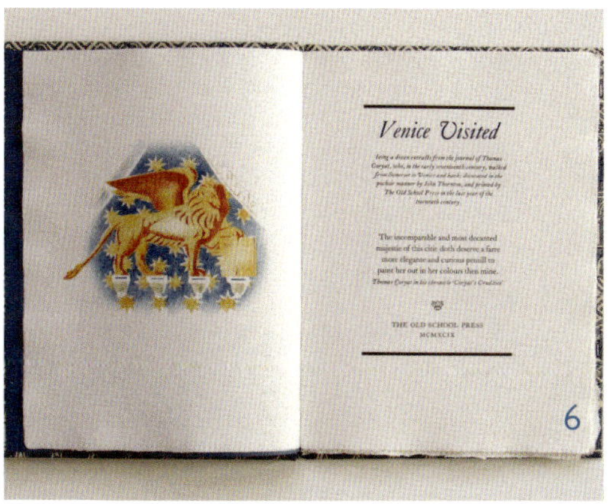

6

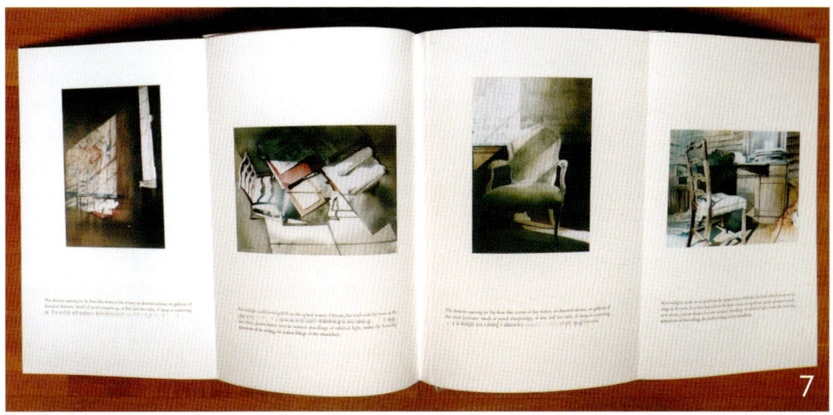
7

Pauline Pearce

exmoorpauline@hotmail.co.uk
www.paulinepearce.co.uk

At some stage during every body of work Pauline Pearce will produce an Artists' Book. Occasionally the book concept comes first, but mostly it develops from the nature of the work evolving through drawing, painting, collage or print. Sometimes they focus on one small part of the whole, other times there can be a whole series of inter-related books.

Each book has a tactile, intimate and fascinating content, whether viewed as part of the larger body of work or on its own. The pleasure for Pauline, is that each book should be like opening Pandora's box: never knowing what you will find.

Book commissions undertaken. Workshops available.

1
Tree Book
23 x 23 cm
Concertina spine: single sheet page attachments: folding sections, hand drawn cover removable, dust jacket.

2
Swallows
12 x 16 cm
Multi-case: hand made paper pages: hand printed images and text: book cloth cover: hand printed detail.

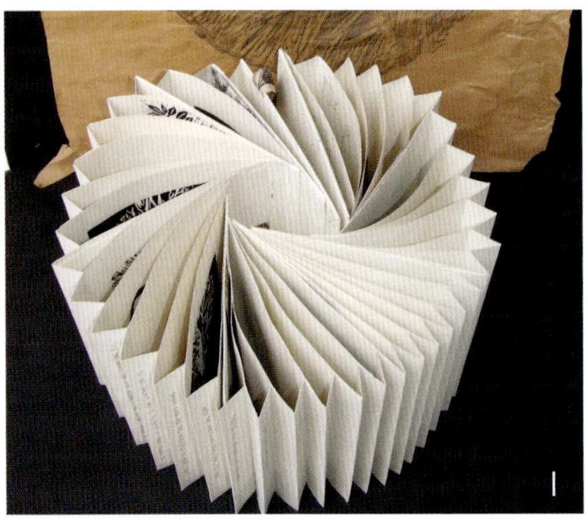
1

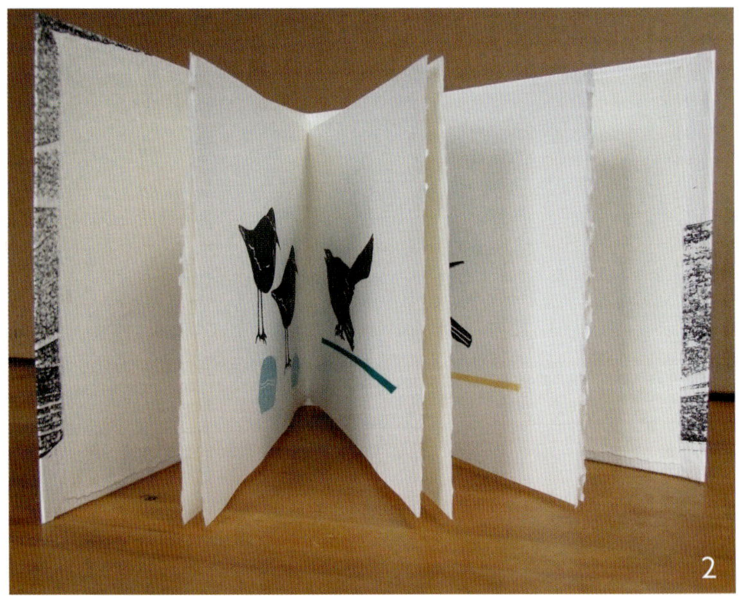
2

Rowena Pearce

qseddon@me.com

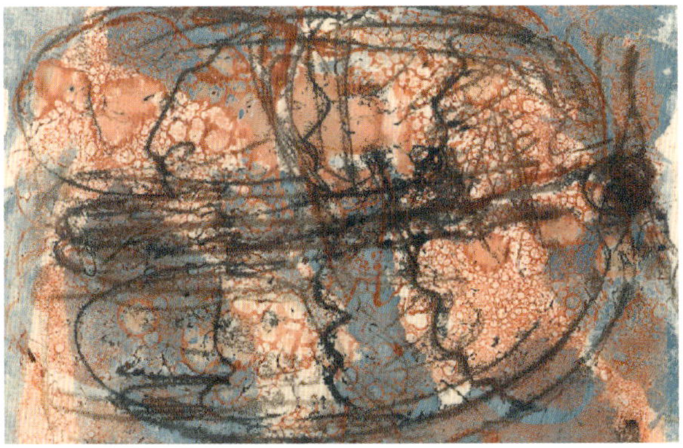

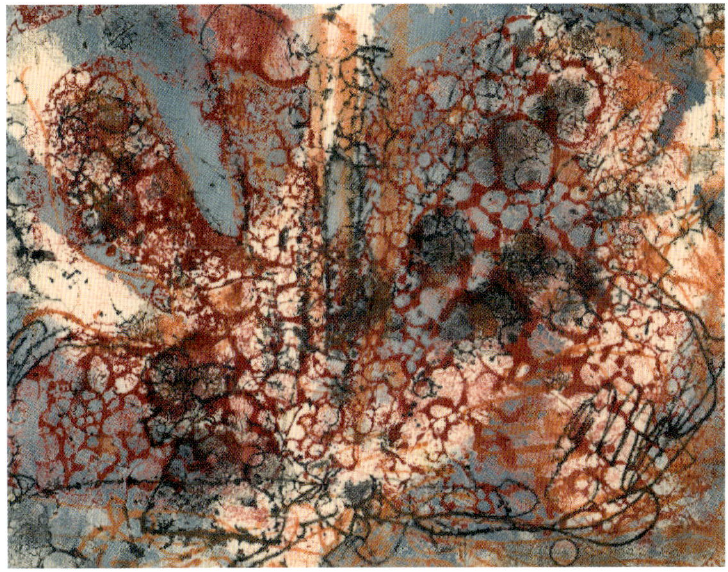

Moth Dreaming
A5
Monoprints - oil on Himalayan paper
Edition of 20

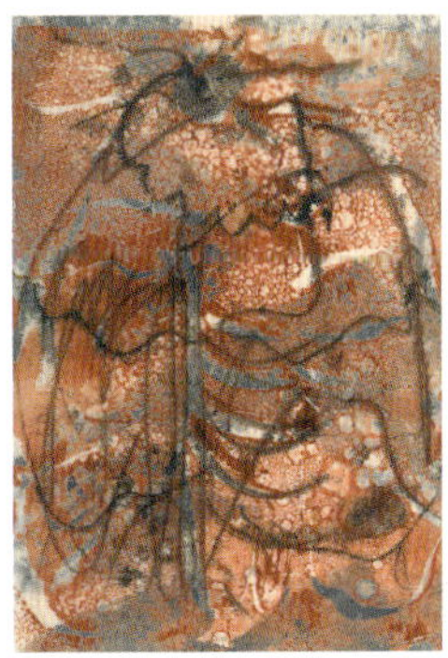

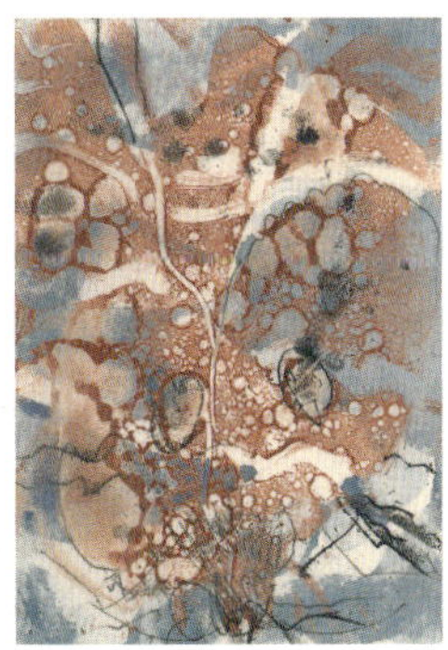

Anne Rook
M.M. Visual Catering

annerook27@yahoo.co.uk
www.annerook.net

1
Penelope's Weaves
2011 18 x 19 cm
Inkjet prints on drawing paper, stitched binding, printed canvas ends covers, edition 10

2
A book of sixteen pears
2013 16 x 16 cm
Concertina book, archival inkjet prints on Hahnemühle fine art paper, printed canvas end covers, edition 20

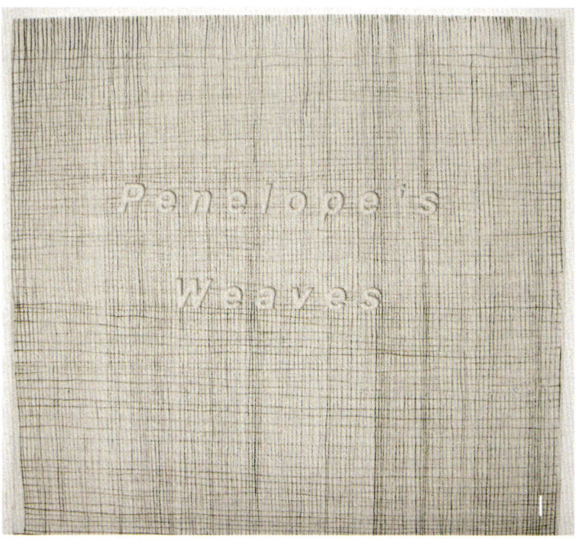

1

In 'Apple-Haiku' and 'Virtual Orchard' fruit labels hint wittily at the economics of global agriculture. 'the book of sixteen pears' is a playful comment on supermarket culture and Jeremy Bentham's dual principle of utility; it is a wondering about eating, growing and selling pears; a collecting of 'utilitarian' fruits.

A landscape of huts suggests the different political, social and geographical contexts in which we sometimes have to live, 'Habitats-Shanti'.

In 'Penelope's Weaves', a poem and twenty drawings imagine Penelope's state of mind while she waits for Ulysses. The colourful and often strange brand names of alcoholic drinks are listed beside some of the plants used to make them. These lists read like strange poems and accompany illustrations derived from 19th century herbals, 'Herbarium'.
Books are digitally printed, bound by hand. They are part of a multimedia practice.

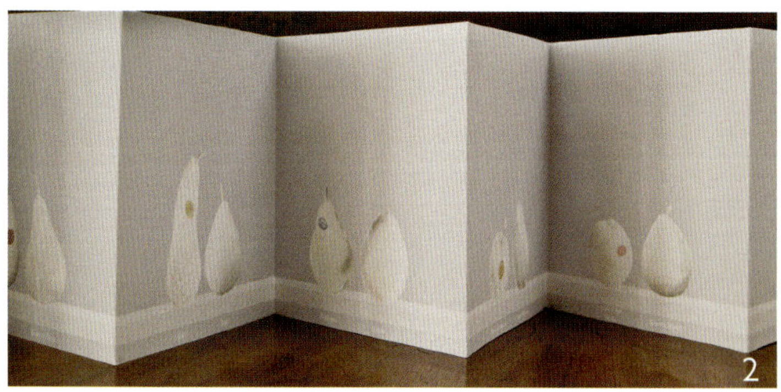
2

3
Twelve Journeys 2012
12.5 x 116 cm unfolded. Concertina book, archival inkjet print on drawing paper, watercolour paper end covers, edition 20

4
Apple Haiku 2009
26 x 26 cm approx. Octagonal folding book, inkjet prints on tracing paper, drawing paper and calico, edition 10

5
Herbarium 2008
15 x 17 cm. Inkjet prints on drawing paper, 12 loose double pages in folded cover, edition 30

6
Virtual Orchard 2009
29.5 x 136 cm unfolded. Concertina book, archival inkjet print on Epson fine art paper, edition 10

7
Habitats - Shanti 2012
40 x 60 cm unfolded. Concertina book, archival inkjet print on Epson fine art paper, edition 5

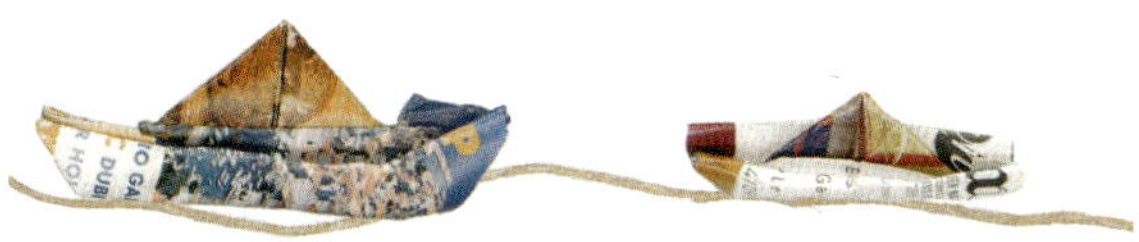

Dominican Priory Museum Dubrovnik 2004 — 'Poussin et Moise' Musée des Gobelins Paris 2012

3

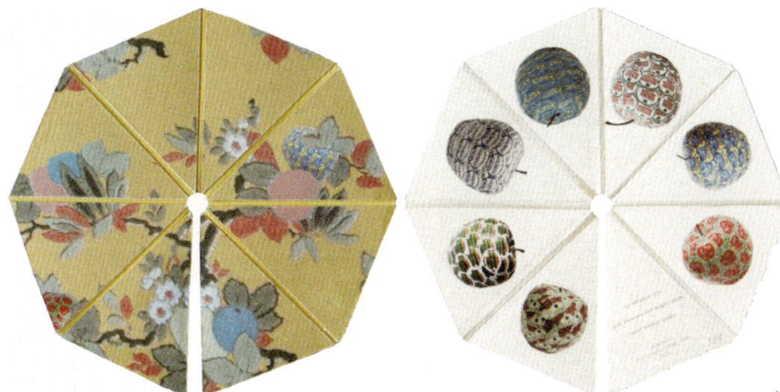

4

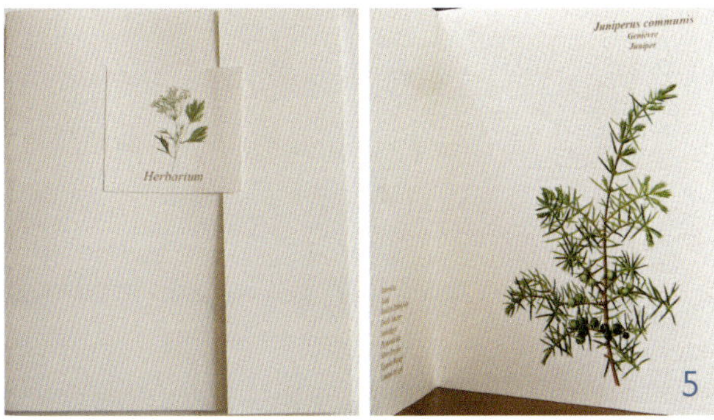

5

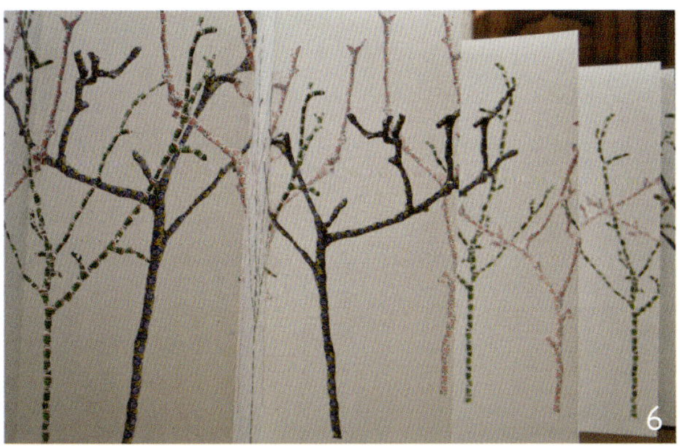

6

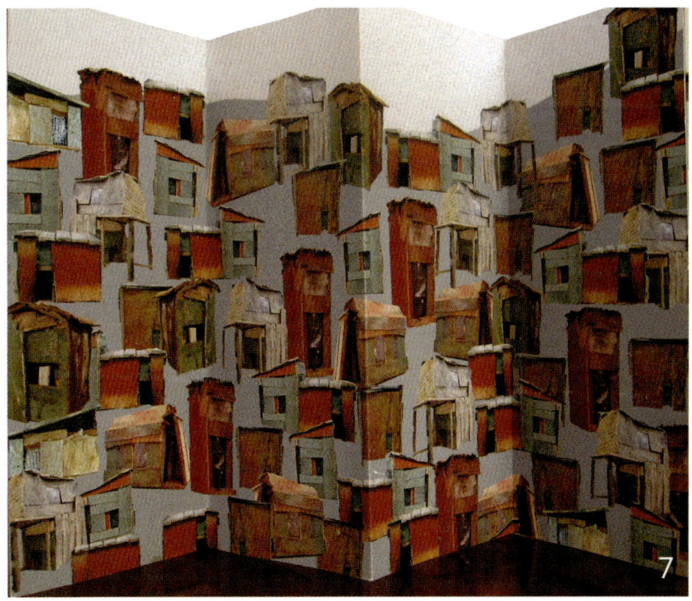

7

Chris Ruston

Chrisruston@btinternet.com
www.Chrisruston.com

1
Winters Rages
30 x 28 cm
Board, various Himalayan papers, painted, inks, gold leaf, stitched, inkjet printed text.

2
Fire - The True Edge of Creation
37 x 25 cm
Board, Fabriano watercolour paper, hand painted, inks, double concertina fold, stitched.

3
Ice - Ripples Held in a Slumber of Blue
19 x 22 cm
Board, Fabriano watercolour paper, hand painted, inks, gesso, concertina fold.

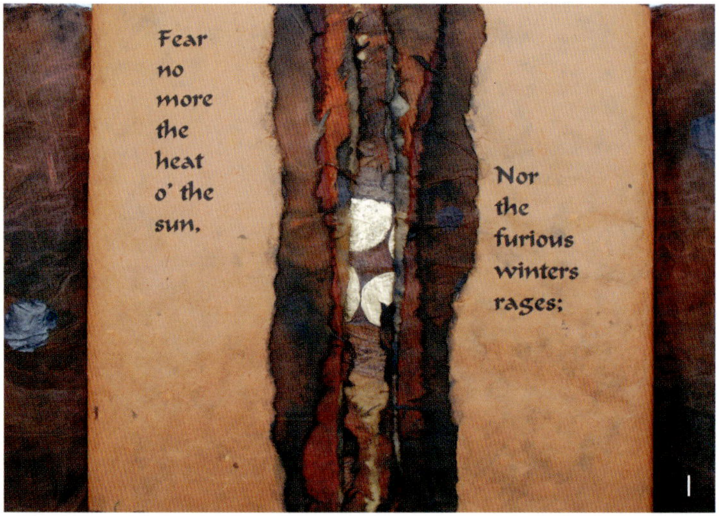

1

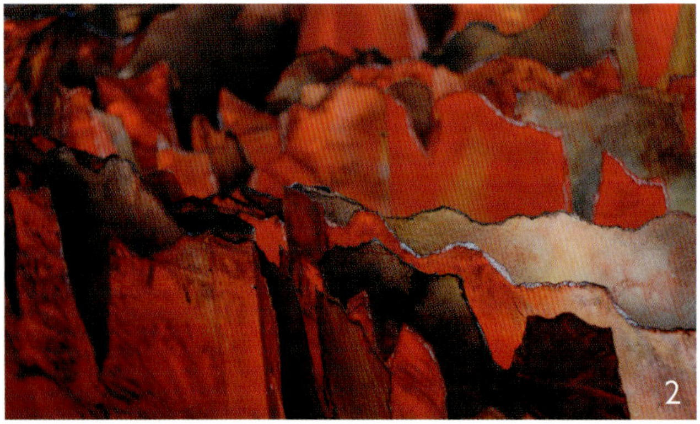
2

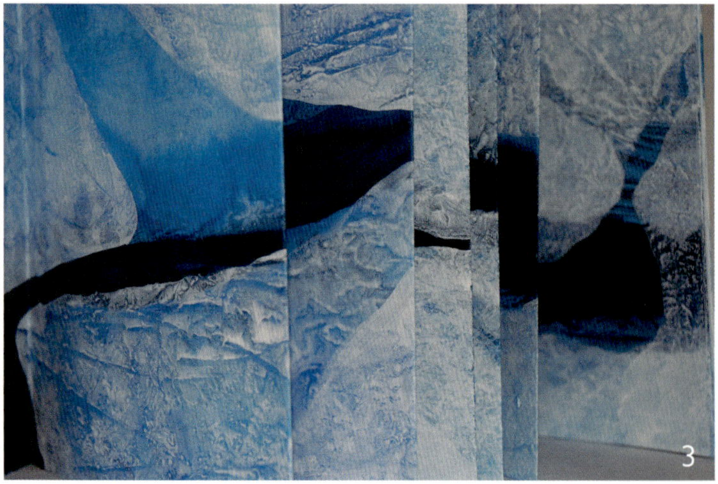
3

Toni Rutherford
Littlebits Books

Littlebitsbooks@aol.com
www.littlebitsbooks.net

1
Beyond reach and function.
8 x 8 x 6 cm
Lasercut plywood box, surrounds a single section leather bound book 3 x 2 cm

2
Shhhh... It's a secret...
11 x 8 cm Coptic binding, handmade paper, cover, holding a secret. Sealed red postal wax; dipped in white wax until only a small window of the cover shows.

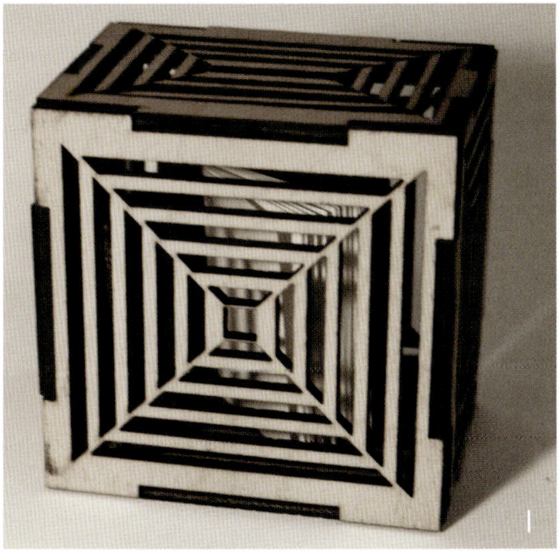
1

Toni Rutherford challenges how we view books within today's society. Are some books too precious to be viewed or read, becoming locked away in an environmentally controlled room with no access. Does this render those books obsolete taking away their original function and purpose? Toni's handmade books are then further treated or locked away behind a fancy façade to show the limited function of a book that has no access to a reader.

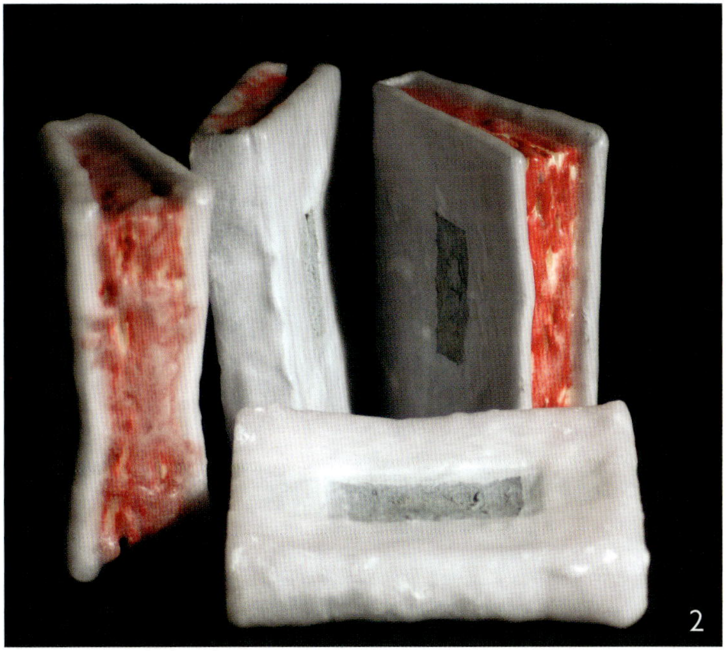
2

Sue Shaw

sue@see-kay.co.uk
www.see-kay.co.uk

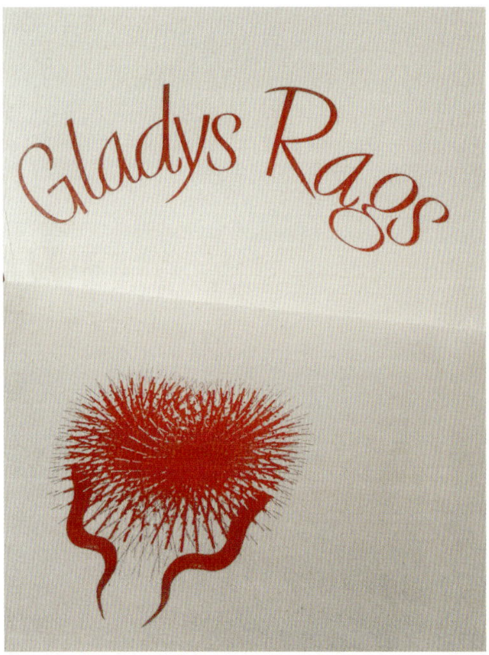

Gladys Rags is a play on words. The book features imaginary textiles (rags), her domestic life and the fact that she annoys her husband (rags). The verse was written in response to the practice of hiding money for "running away" if in an unhappy marriage.

Her mother had said, on the night of her wedding,
Have you got your running away money?
So she had sewn into her cloth a lining of safety
with running stitches and shillings.
As cloth turned to rags and tongue lashings became lashings,
she sewed, satin & blanket & cross & shillings.
It came long overdue to take her money,
But after so much sewing it seemed unfair
to unpick her home,
so she sewed him with stab stitches and crumpled him up.

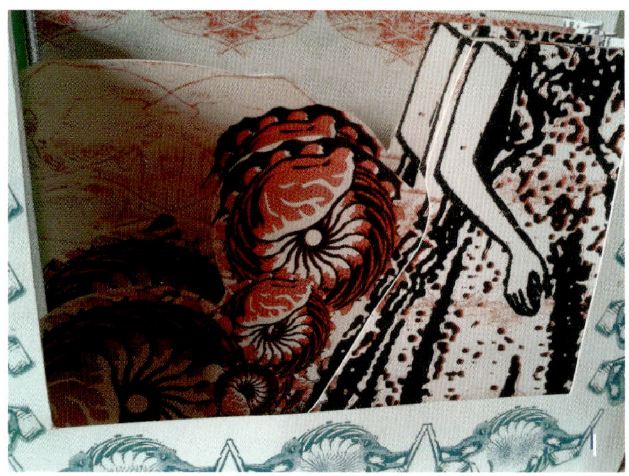

1
Wedding

2 & 3
Washing

4
Close up

5
Ironing

The book is constructed from 3 colour risographs, it is slightly smaller than A5. Each page telescopes out to add another dimension to viewing the pages.

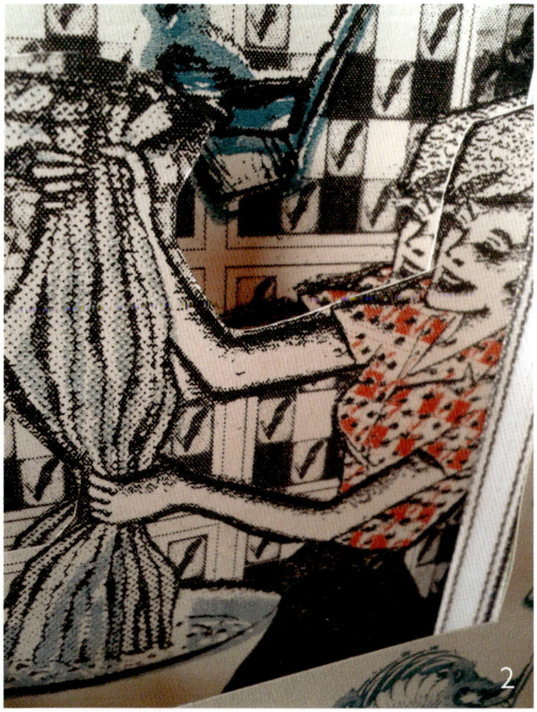

2

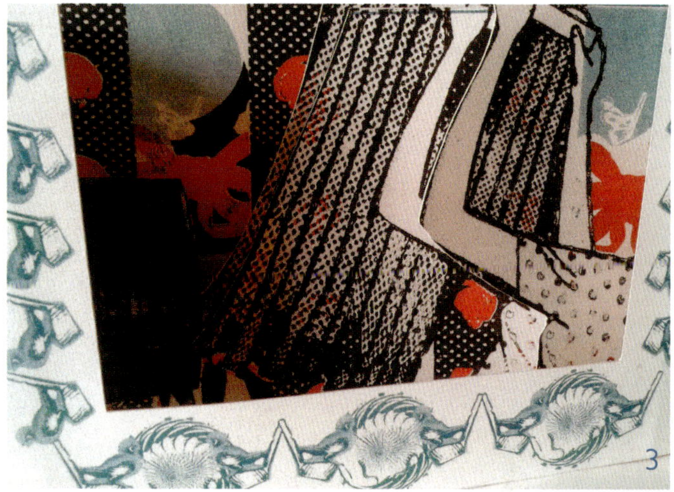

3

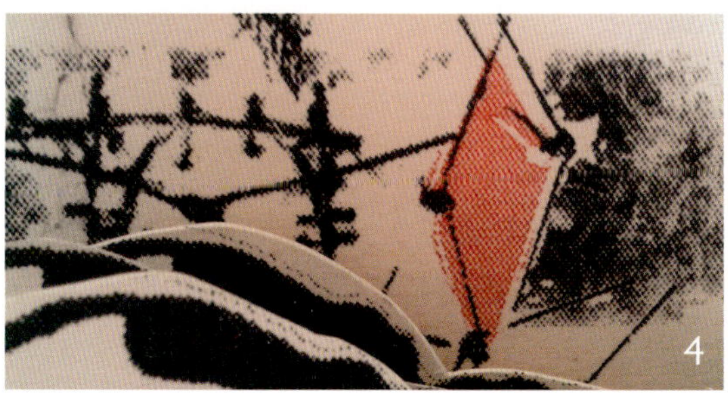

4

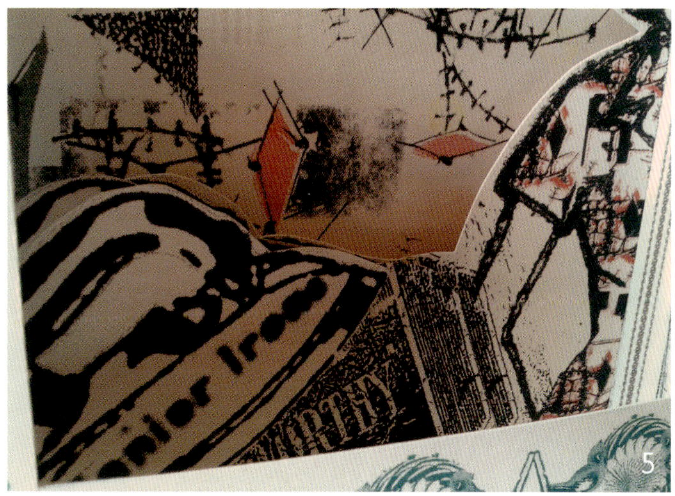

5

Shed Press Publications

shedpress@london.com
www.shedpress.org

Amelie Genestine-Charlton and Jessica Jane Charleston founded Shed Press Publications in 2010 on Cheshire Street, in London.

Their first publication Next-to-Nothing, a book of 9 poems by David Charleston, was launched in December 2011. Next-to-Nothing is a limited edition of 102 (now sold out), set and printed on their Adana Press. Each page is hand-torn and each book is lovingly hand-bound. The book also contains five original photographs that have been hand-printed in their Dark-Shed.

Shed Press create books that are original and hand-made using their Adana presses, flower presses, Dark-Sheds, Lithographic press, paper and thread. Shed Press strive to build books that are irreplaceably wonderful.

1
67/102
Limited numbered edition, hand torn paper.

2
Next-to-Nothing
Title page of book, letterpress, section sewn, hand bound. (Book size: 20 x 11 cm)

3
Blindness Approaches
Poem & hand-printed photograph. (Photo 5 x 8 cm)

1

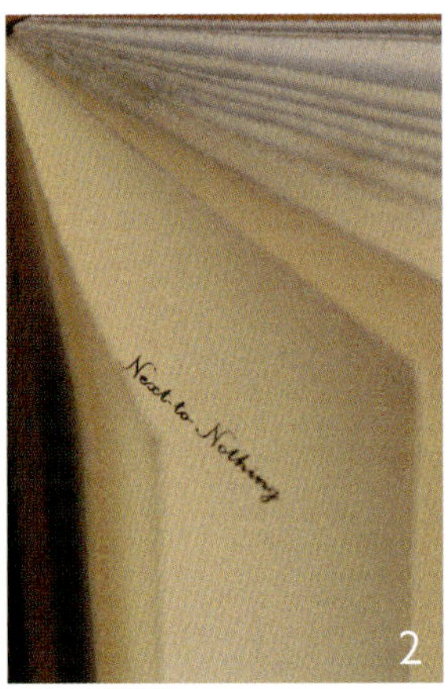

2

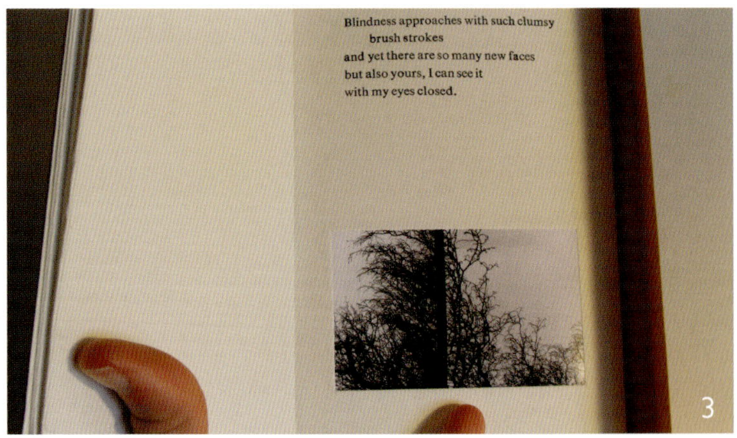

3

Gwen Simpson

gwensimpson@me.com

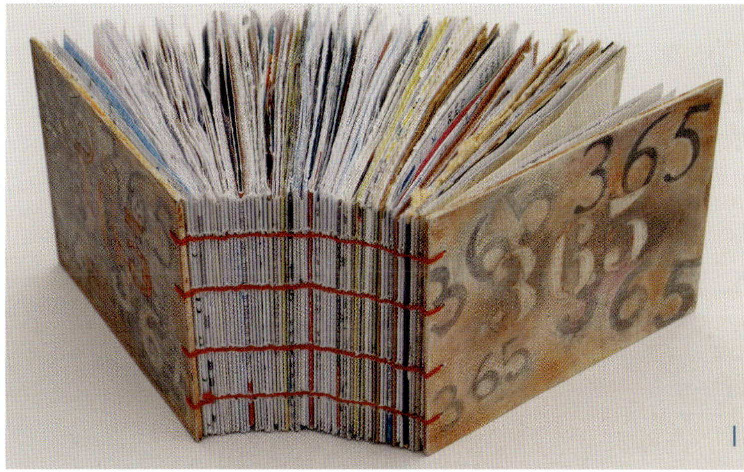

1

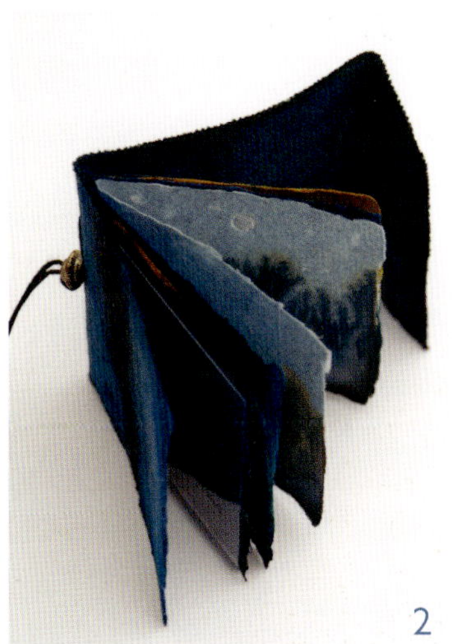

2

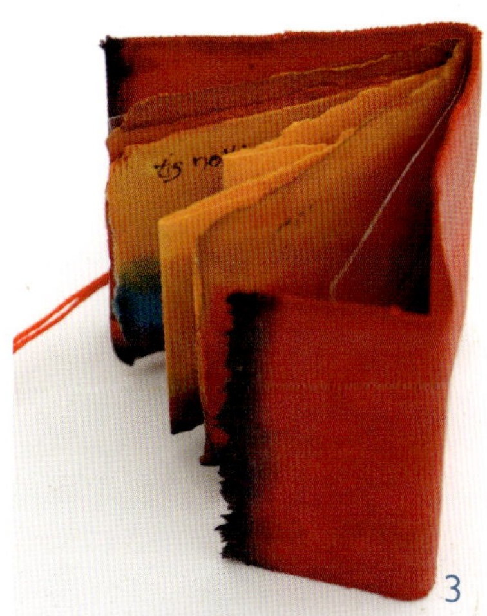

3

1
365, 2013
10.5 x 9 cm
Found and discarded ephemera. Coptic stitch, cover boards, hand incised numerals.

2
Wild landscapes, 2013
7 x 6.5 cm
Pamphlet sewn, waxed blue canvas cover, hand made paper, ink.

3
Magic Shadow
7 x 7 cm
Pamphlet sewn, waxed red canvas cover, hand made paper, ink.

Graham Smith

g.prints@virginmedia.com
www.gfsmith.net

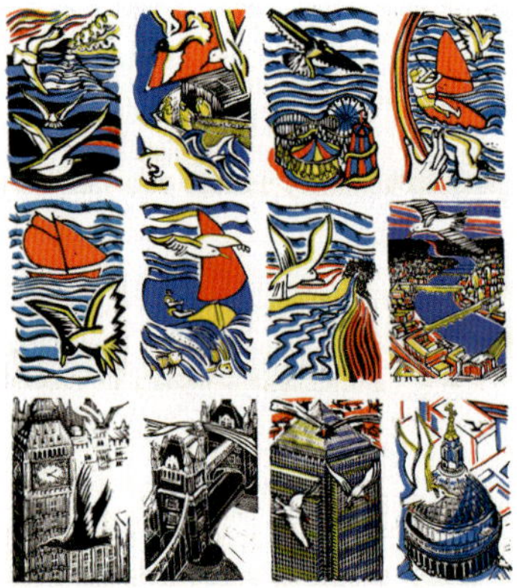

1

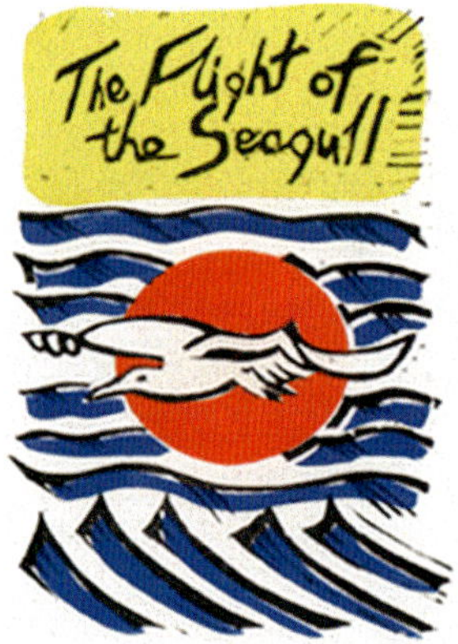

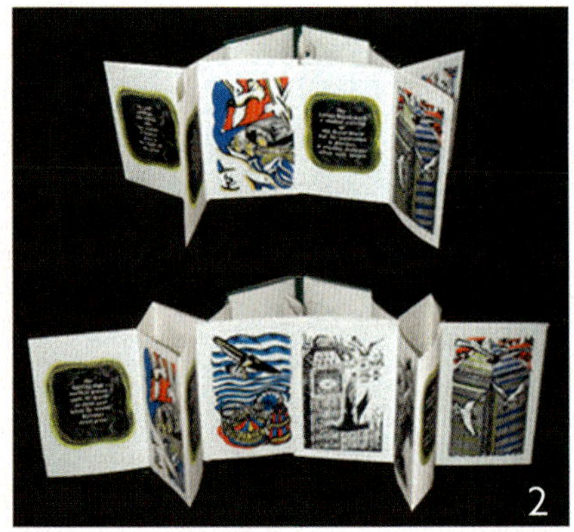

2

1
The Flight of The Seagull
A concertina book
22 X 16 cm
Images printed by hand lino block & stencil.
Text by silkscreen.

2
The Flight of The Seagull
Prints

3
IKON
H15 X W22 X D26 cm
MDF covered by block printed paper, Lino-block images, mirrors and metal hinge

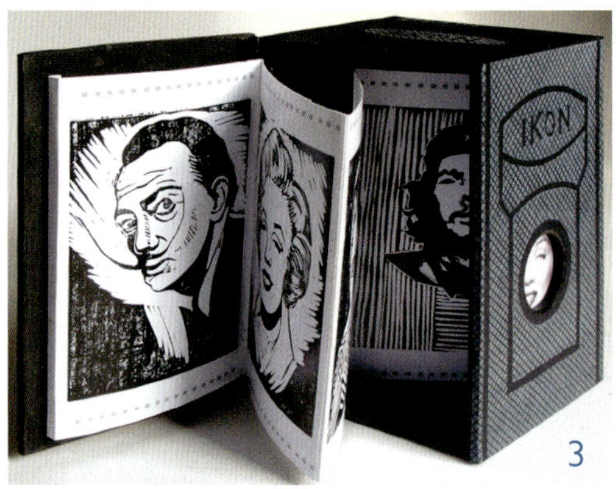

3

4
Rudyard Kiplings
The Ballad of the Cars
26 X 38 cm Images hand printed by vinyl block. A concertina book. Text by silkscreen.

5
Images from The Ballad of the Cars by Rudyard Kipling

6
From 'Oak to Iron' *commemorating shipbuilding in Sunderland*

7
A visual history of Sunderland FC

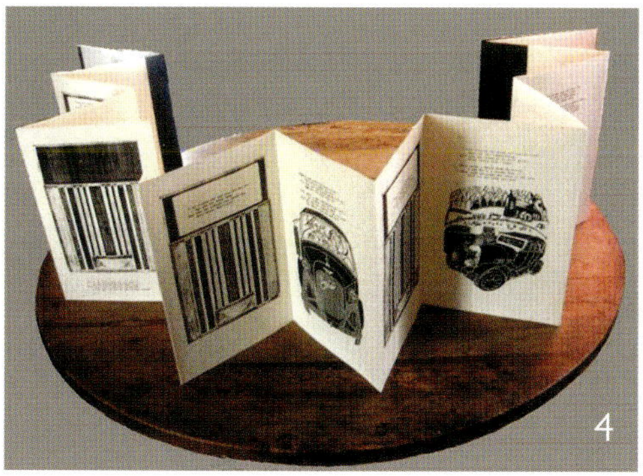

4

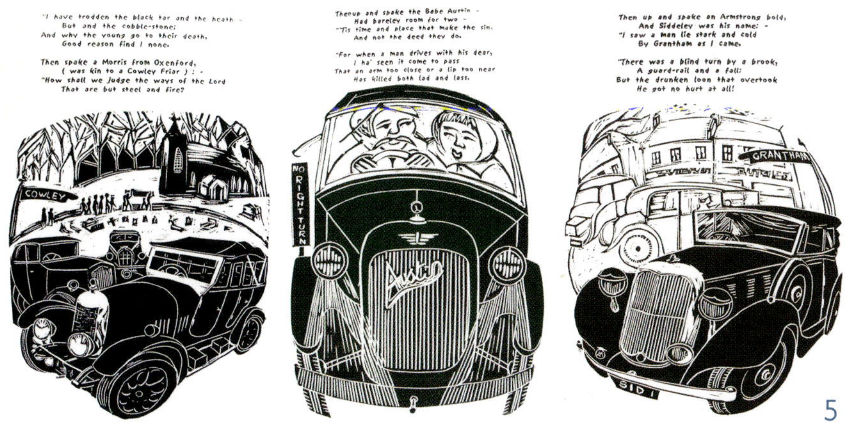

5

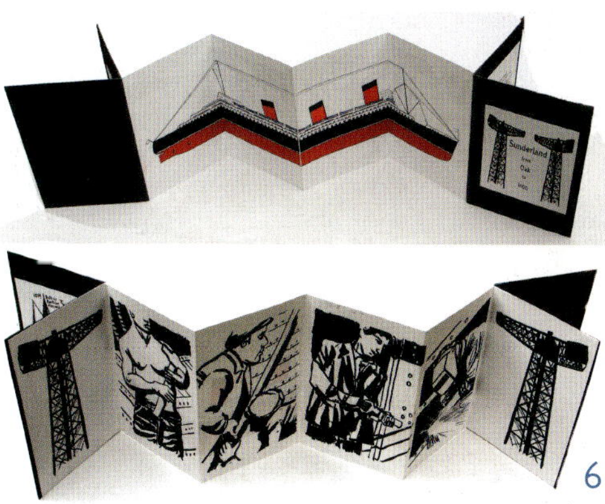

6

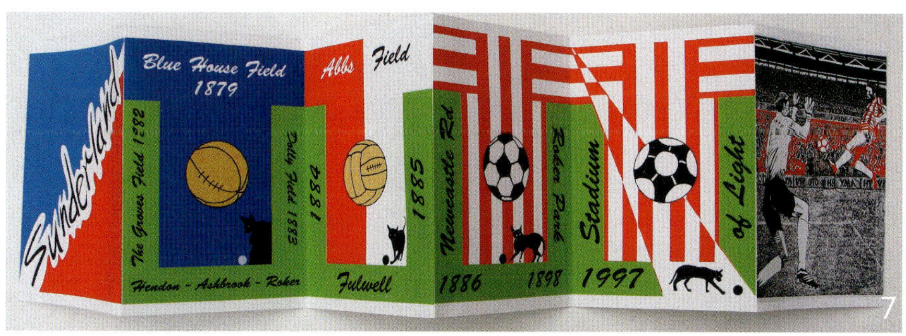

7

Jenny Smith

jenny@jennysmith.org.uk
www.jennysmith.org.uk
www.theartistbookgroup.org.uk
www.edinburghlaserstudio.org.uk.

1
what is the best advice you have been given?
15 x 15 cm closed
digitally printed & laser cut papers

2
book of beads
16 x 16 cm closed
laser cut, screen printed Somerset paper

Framed within the parameters of Zen philosophy, Jenny Smith's work foregrounds the relationship between traditional fine art methodologies and new digital technologies. She draws using meditative, repetitive hand-rendered processes, and then develops the work using laser cutting and etching, Jenny's artist books invite interaction from the viewer, changing when handled, or viewed from different angles and as the light changes around then.

Jenny gained a B.A (hons) 1st class Drawing and Painting, from Duncan of Jordanstone College of Art, Dundee and an MA in Multi-Disciplinary Print, UWE, Bristol. She exhibits nationally and internationally and has work held in collections worldwide including the Tate Library and National Galleries of Scotland. Based in Edinburgh, she set up and runs The Artist Book Group and The Edinburgh Laser Cutting Studio.

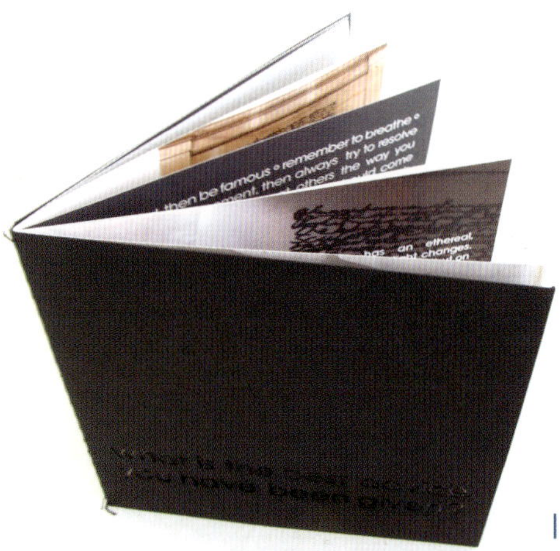

1

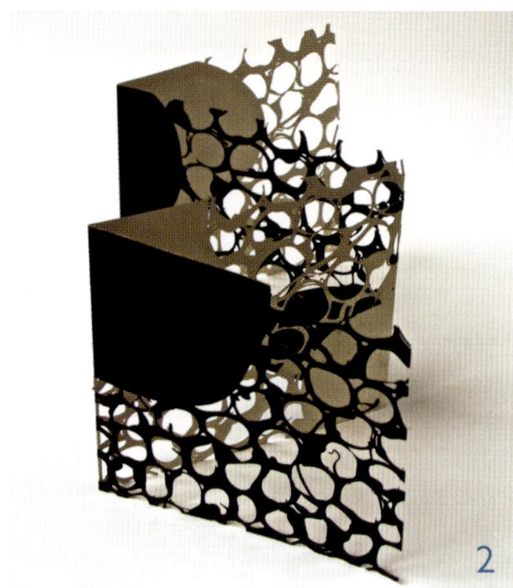

2

3
silent syllables
16 x 16 cm closed
laser cut, screen printed Somerset paper

4
untitled
6 x 6 cm closed
laser cut, screen printed Somerset paper

5
untitled - square
16 x 16 cm closed
laser cut, screen printed Somerset paper

6
little black book
16 x 16 cm closed
laser cut, screen printed Somerset paper

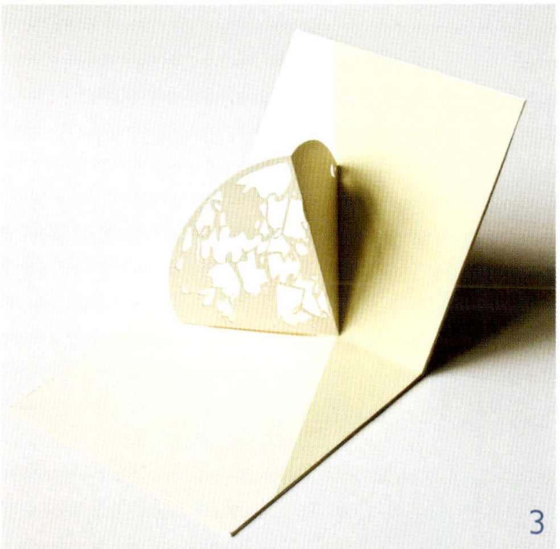
3

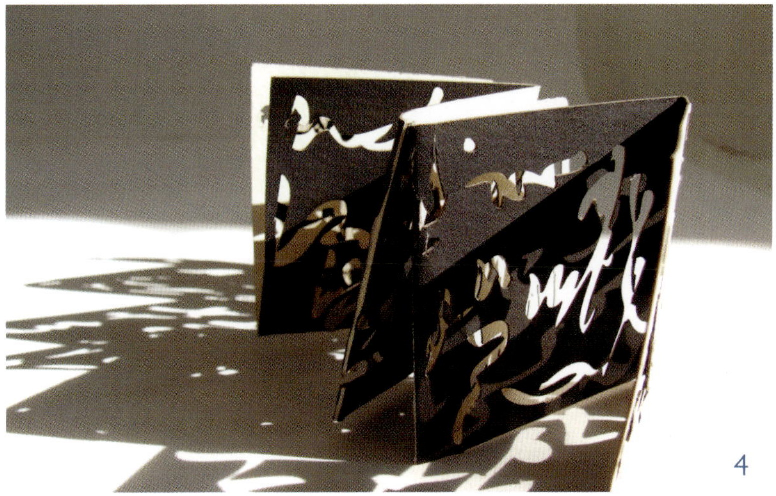
4

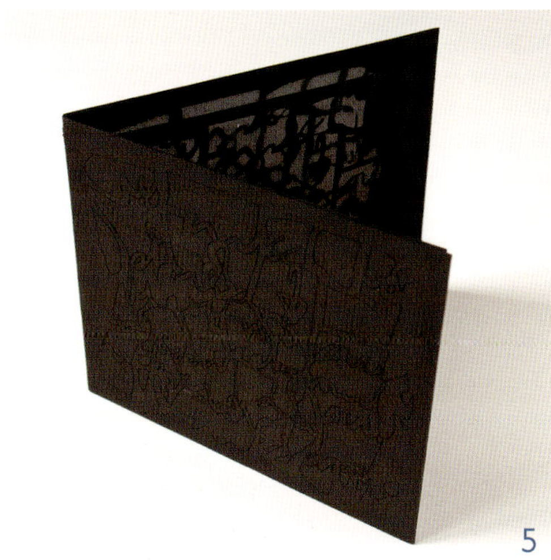
5

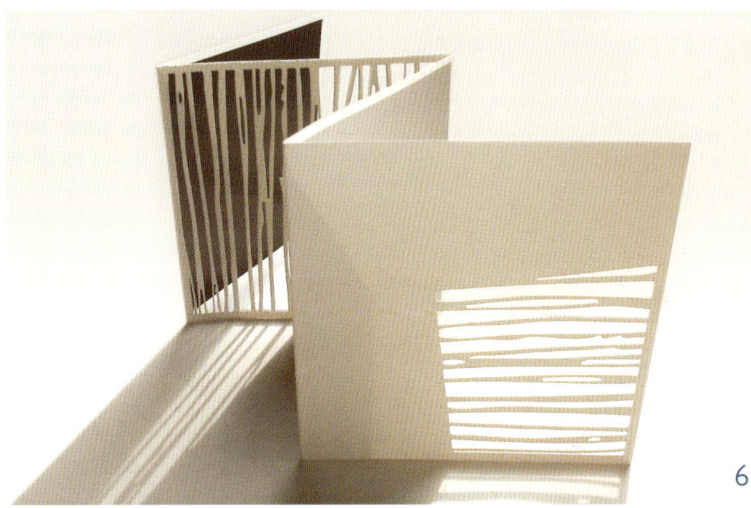
6

Alix Swan

alixswan@hotmail.com
www.facebook.com/alixswan.
littlebitsofprintythings

Alix Swan is a fine art bookmaker who makes quirky and amusing handmade books, objects and 3D-illustrations to represent vintage stories, rhymes and sayings which she offers as an original twist on the traditional to bring reminiscence, rediscovery and joy.

Her works draw on an eclectic mix of textiles, paper, print and graphics and she cuts, sews, assembles and binds by hand. She often works on a small, even miniature scale but always with a keen eye for detail and finish.

Alix's home and studio in the heart of England is a treasure trove of found and second-hand materials together with a computer, digital camera and four old typewriters. There she conjures new and old memories for those with a love of stories.

1
Witches House
9 x 5 x 2 cm
Illustrated & hand cut pull-out; paper & print

2
Interactive Wallpiece. Thumbelina
19 x 15.5 x 13.5 cm
3D illustration with music box & handmade book; mixed media

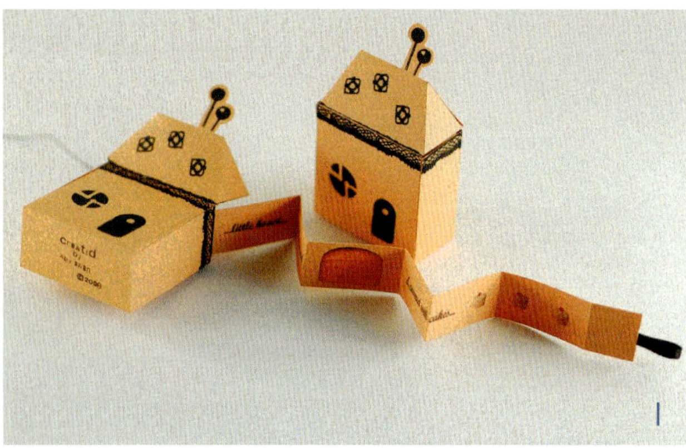

1

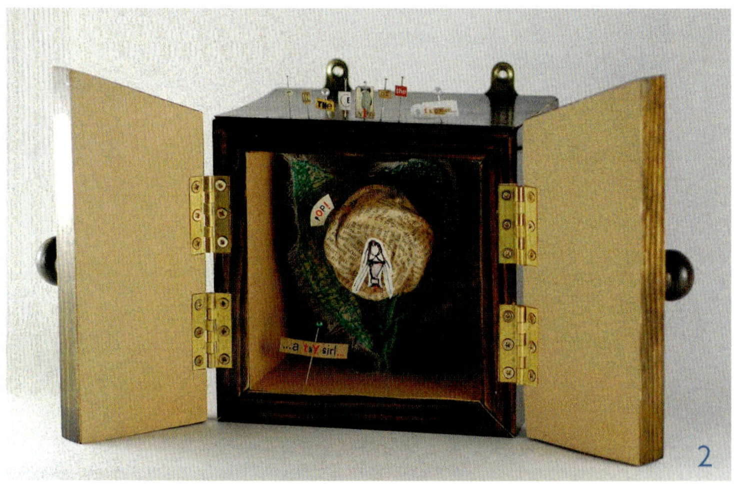

2

3
Little Riding-Hood
11 x 2.5 x 8 cm
Illustrated & traditionally hand-bound book; paper, print, threads & treads

4
Dust Jacket Books
sizes vary. Illustrated & traditionally hand-bound books; paper, print, threads & treads

5
Shoebox.
Alice's Adventures in Wonderland
5.5 x 2.5 x 5 cm
'Kie-Kie Book' & handmade shoes; mixed media

6
Interactive Story House.
Little Riding-Hood
47 x 15.2 x 42 cm
3D illustration with music box & handmade book; mixed media

Alix Swan

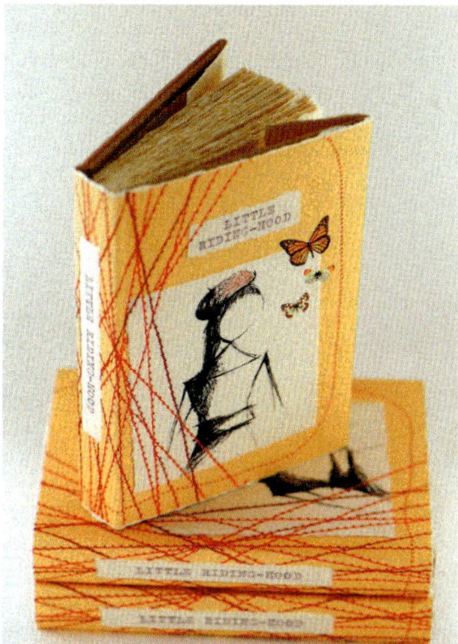

3

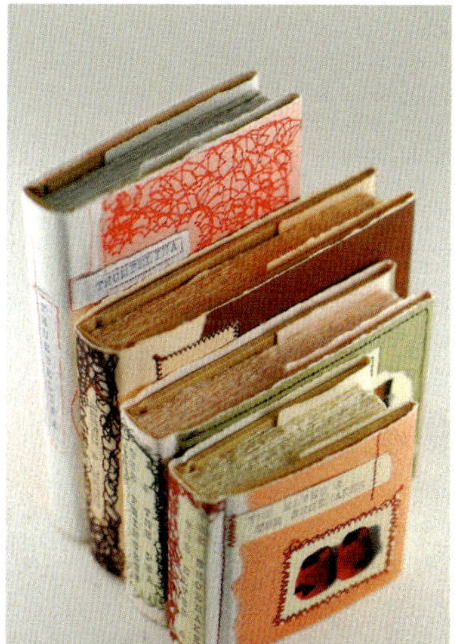
4

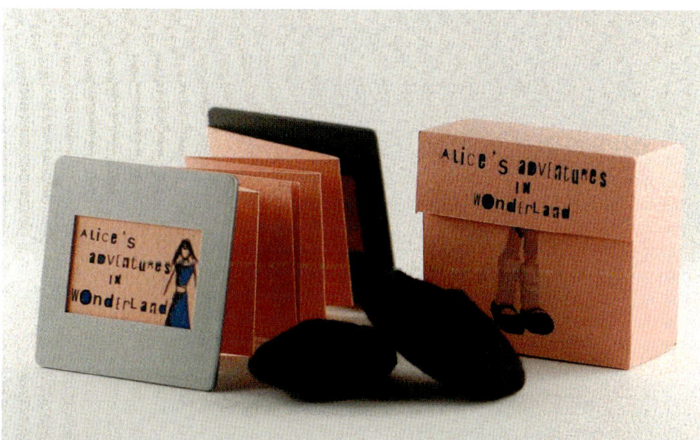

5

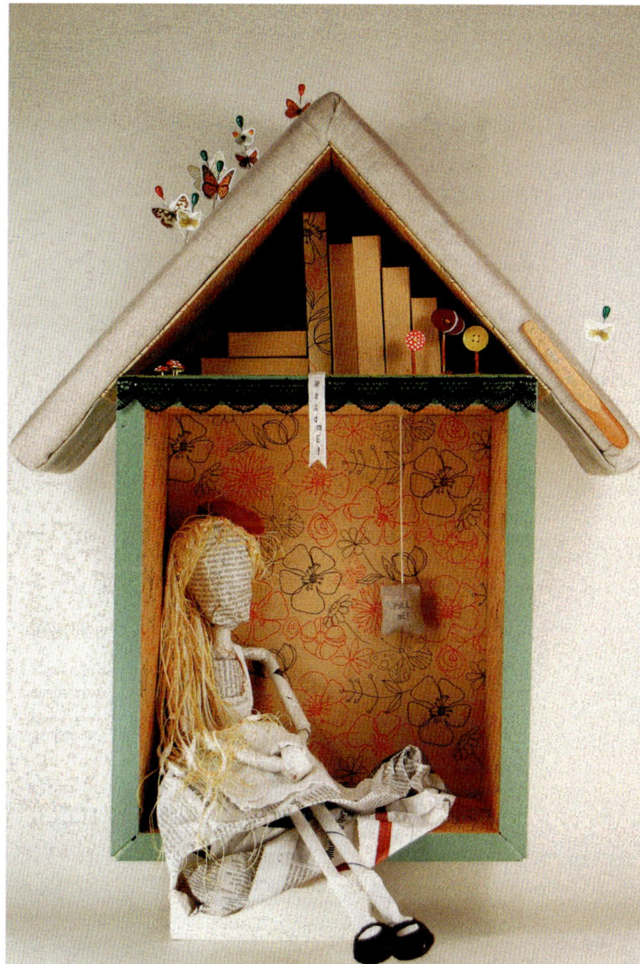
6

Lola Swain

lolaswain@yahoo.co.uk
www.lolaswainpottery.com

1
Marbled Sketchbook
10.5 x 10.5 x 1.5 cm
Hand marbled and bound 130gsm acid free cartridge paper

2
The Monarch
10.3 x 10.3 x 2.1 cm
Clay tiles with burnished slip, paper, letraset text, hemp string

Lola Swain is a potter from Leigh on Sea, Essex. With a developing interest in book art she had discovered the ideal opportunity to combine her love of clay and the natural world. It is one that has since grown to encompass other facets of book art including hand paper marbling and book binding.

'The Monarch' is inspired by the butterfly of that name and poem by Ross Gardner. The lines of the poem are printed on each face of the concertinaed paper, requiring the reader to read through the book in a unique and literal way reflecting the sense of movement of the butterfly in flight.

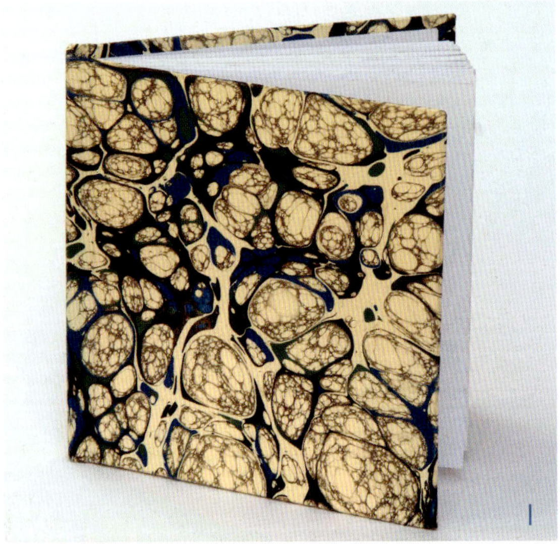

1

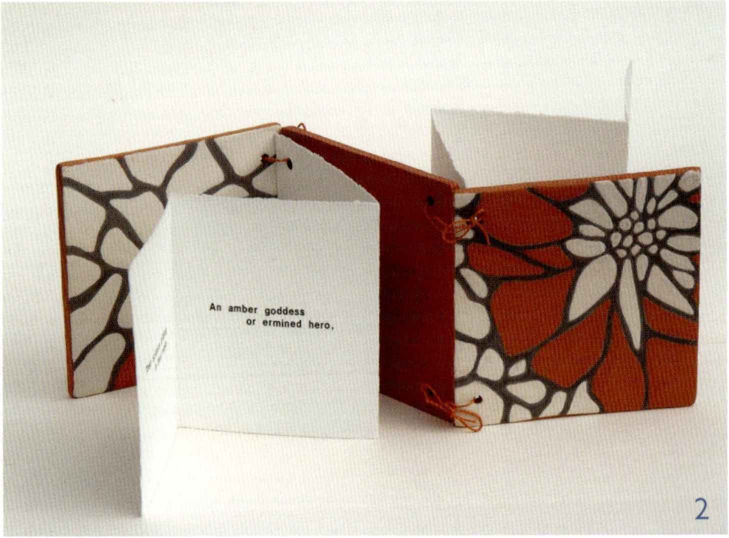

2

Anna Swingland
Hadwin's Books

anna.swingland@gmail.com
www.hadwinsbook.co.uk

Based in Kent, Anna Swingland is the creator of Hadwin's Book. Underlying her work is a fascination for Western traditional binding methods; within these boundaries she experiments to produce a combination of established and playful work.

Her designs can be separated into two approaches; the first is producing practical working books that have a sentimental reflection on neglected objects, such as disused keys or board games. The second is concentrated on gallery pieces that study the concept of the purpose and function of binding; this is usually combined with taboo or controversial subjects. Anna also works on a commission basis and can be contacted though her website.

1
1/4 bound book
12 x 20 cms
Recycled cartridge paper, french stitch, buckram, decorative paper.

2
Banned restriction; My Struggle
17 x 23 cms
1938 text block, book - cloth, marble paper, embossed lettering.

3
Monopoly
26 x 26 cms
Original board game, recycled cartridge paper, french stitch, buckram, ribbon, Monopoly money, player piece

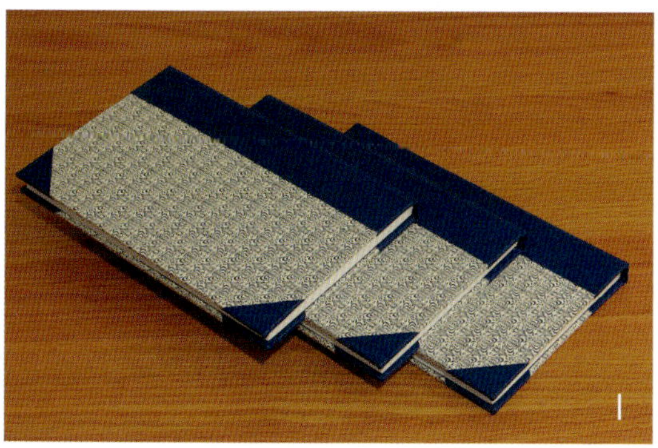

1

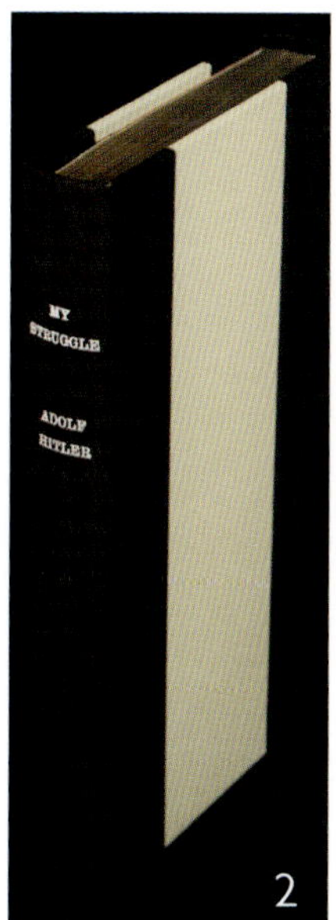

2

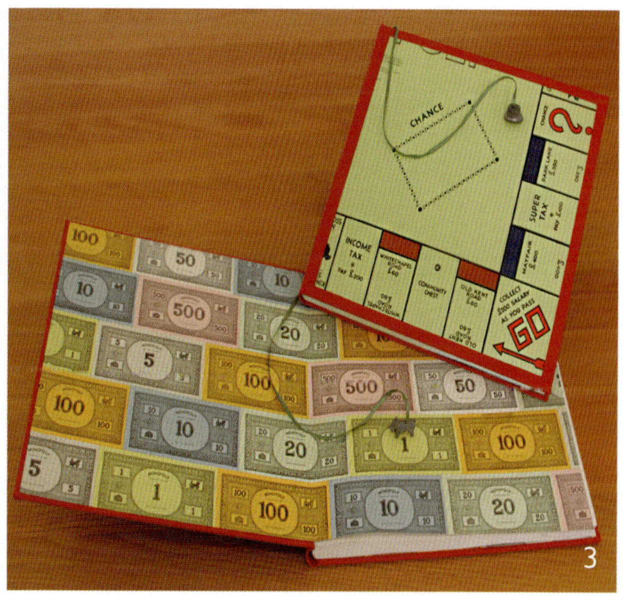

3

Kim Tarpey

art@kimtarpeyaustralia.com
www.kimtarpeyaustralia.com

Kim Tarpey is a British painter, printmaker and ceramicist working in Melbourne Australia. Natural disasters near to home have prompted her to create thematic works that overview community response to environmental concerns.

Learning How to Compromise: this book of Poetry and Prose embodies two suites of etchings, *The Credulous Ones*, 2010 and *Des Pastoral*, 2012. *The Credulous Ones* uses Australian Colonial themes in allegory depicting current attitudes to the indigenous landscape and its creatures. *Des Pastoral* is a look at the tensions that exist in a rural community repairing itself after a disaster. Tarpey has used bees symbolically to represent the domestication of nature; they can be dangerous, like snakes. The native and threatened Teddy Bear Bee also puts in an appearance.

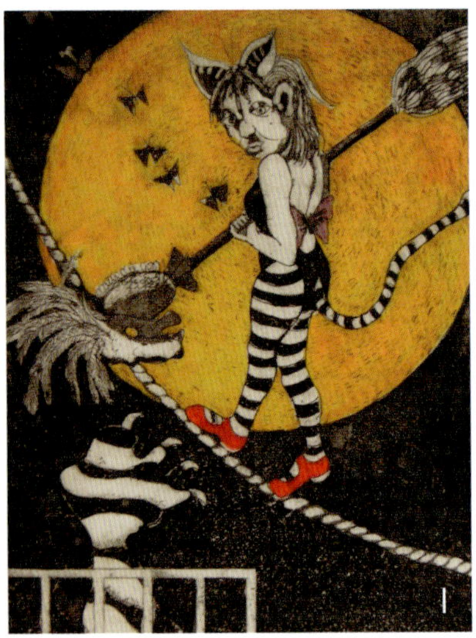

1

1 Learning How to Compromise *34.5 x 24.5 cm Etching, aquatint watercolour on cotton paper*

2 The Bee Dancer *Etching aquatint & water colour 34.5 x 24.5 cm*

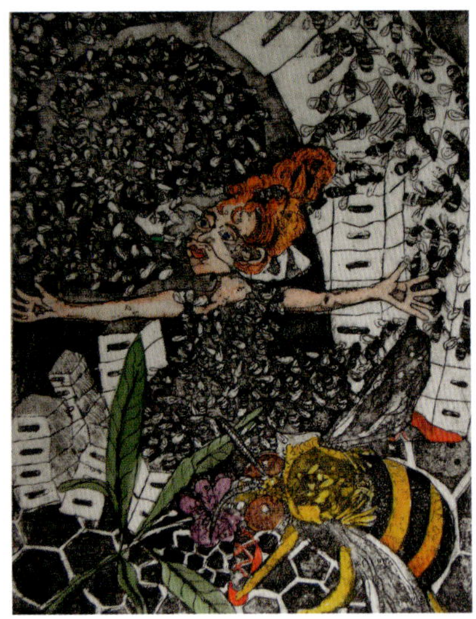

2

3
St Ned
Etching aquatint & watercolour with poem. open page of book 40 x 71 cm

4
Bluey in the Queensland Blues
24.5cm square Etching, aquatint & watercolour on cotton paper

5
Queen Bee
Etching aquatint & watercolour 24.5 square

6
Tails from Grandma
Etching aquatint & watercolour with poem, open book size 40 x 71 cm

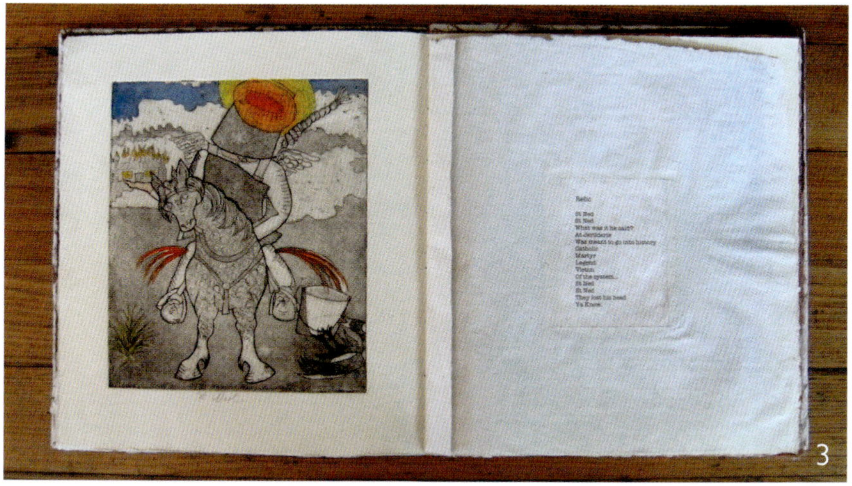

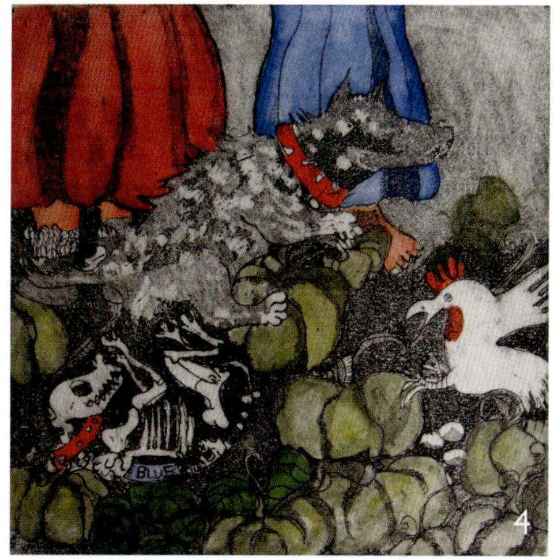

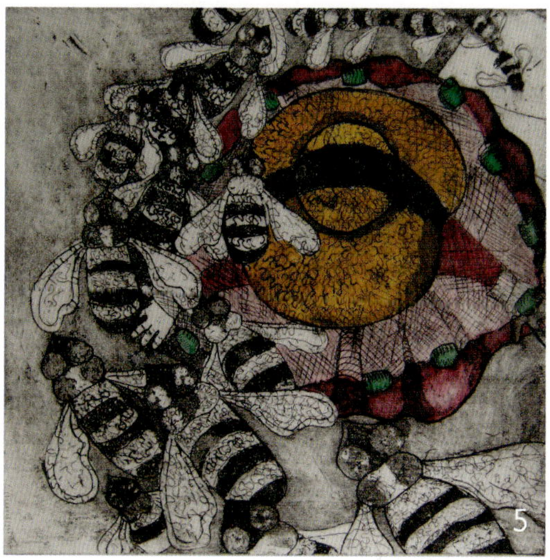

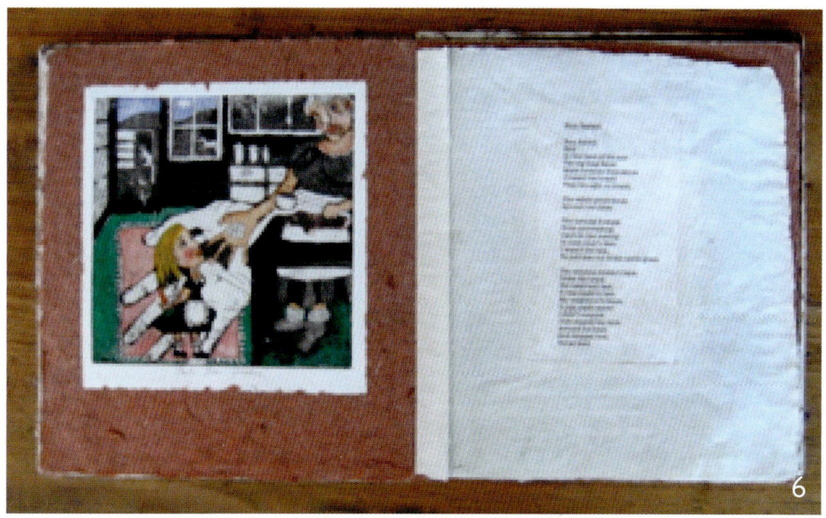

Louise Tett

louisetett@gmail.com
Web: louisetett.blogspot.co.uk

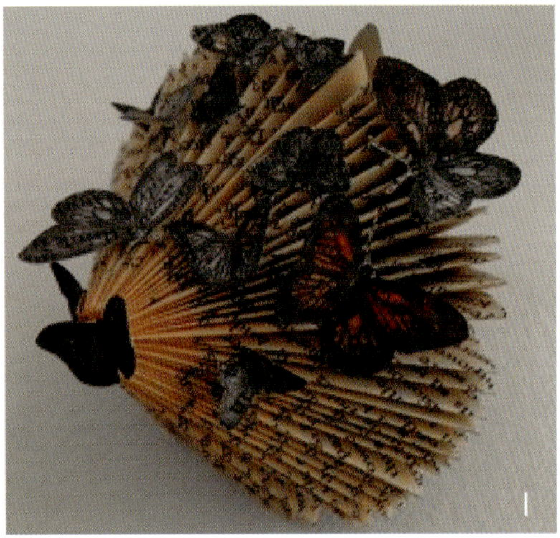

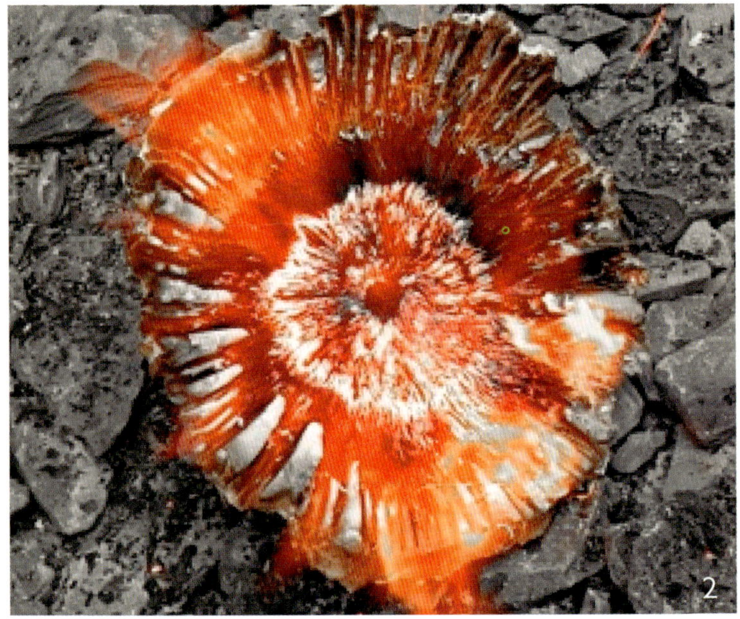

1
Not all those who wander are lost
14 x 20 cm
Diamond folded vintage book, hand cut watercolour painted butterflies

2
Pyre
15 x 10 cm
Burning diamond folded vintage book sculpture, plaster.

3
Poem Yarn
1 x 1 to 3 x 3 cm
Hand cut vintage poems, spun with alpaca fleece.

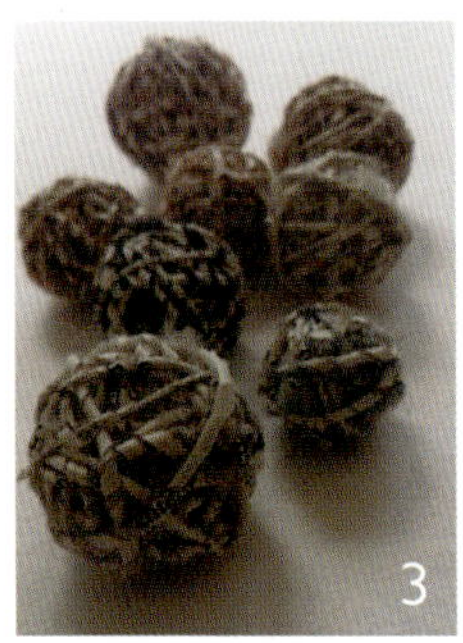

1
The Google-eyed Phoenix Bird
(Britannica britannica}
46ht x 57 x 38 cm
Altered encyclopaedia, the phoenix bird rises from the burnt interior of the discarded book!

2
'Zhen Xian Bao' replica of Chinese folk art book
13 x 24 cm Metallic hand - made papers and traditional Chinese zhezhi paper

3
Rock Book.
Approx 10 x 8 cm
This comment on life has images of rocks and subtle text contained in rocks.

4
Time Passing, a Meditation on the Lessons of Life
16 x 28 cm Examining the effects of life's challenges & possible positive outcomes with complex images and hidden stories.

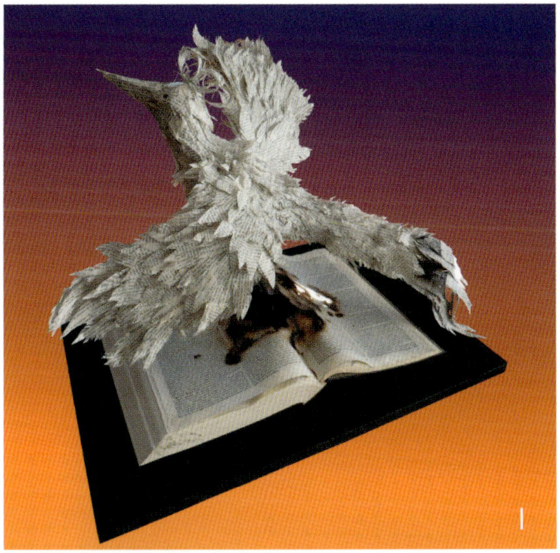
1

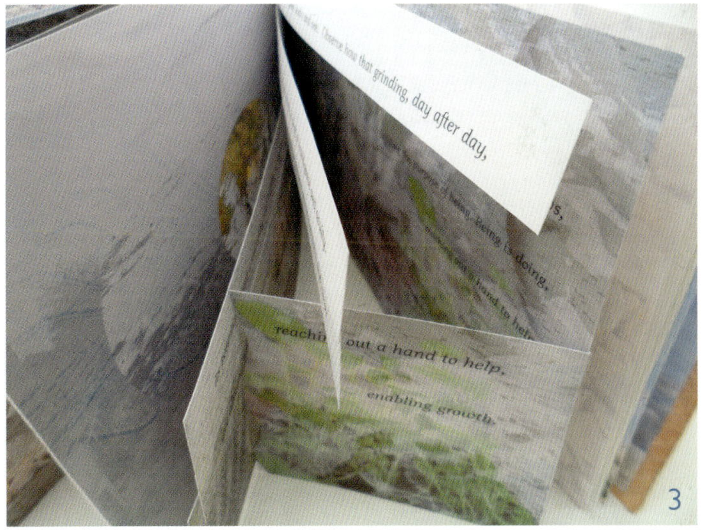

3

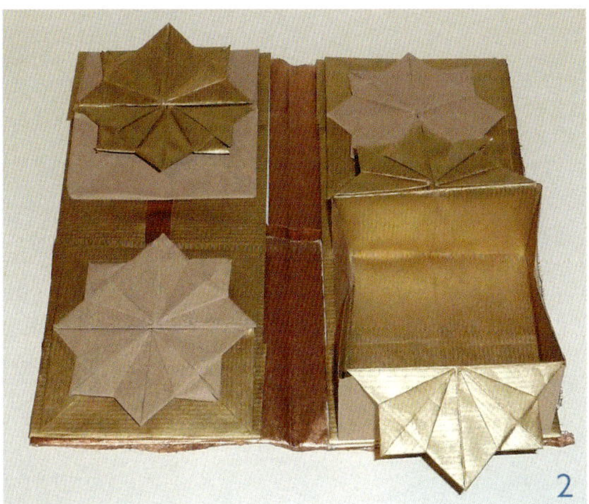
2

1 & 2
Mellie Lane
melanie.lane@virgin.net
www.deckle-edged.com

3 & 4
Wendy J. Allen
allenbookart@yahoo.co.uk
www.allenbookart.co.uk

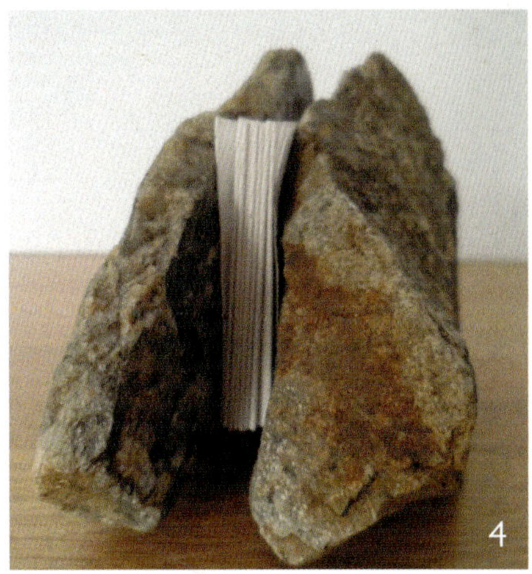
4

Carolyn Trant
parvenu press

carolyn@carolyntrant.co.uk
www.carolyntrant.co.uk

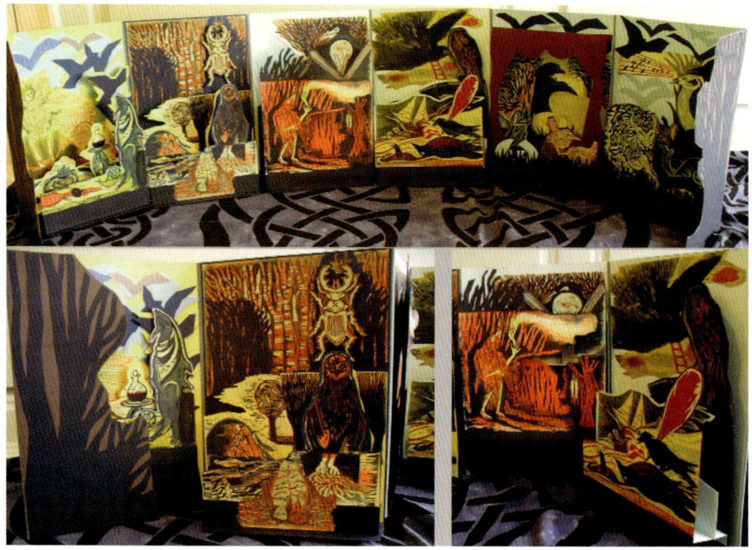

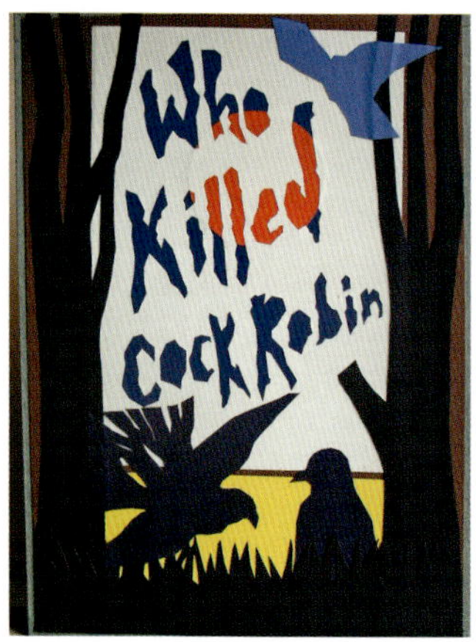

Who Killed Cock Robin
pop-up concertina version
page size 29 x 42 cm stands in a curve, images as opposite page plus coloured card in an illustrated slipcase, up to 6 made to order, signed and dated 2013

Who Killed Cock Robin

First version – double sided concertina format, hand-printed colour woodcut images and text pages 22.5 x 28 cm
Walnut veneer covered boards 17 x 35 cm with hemp tie edition of 13 signed and dated 2012

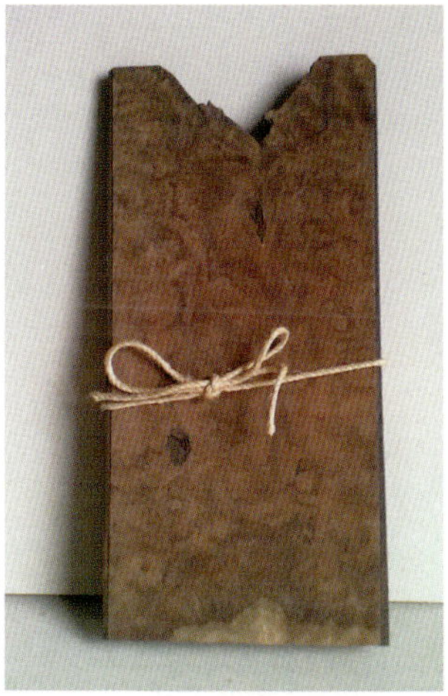

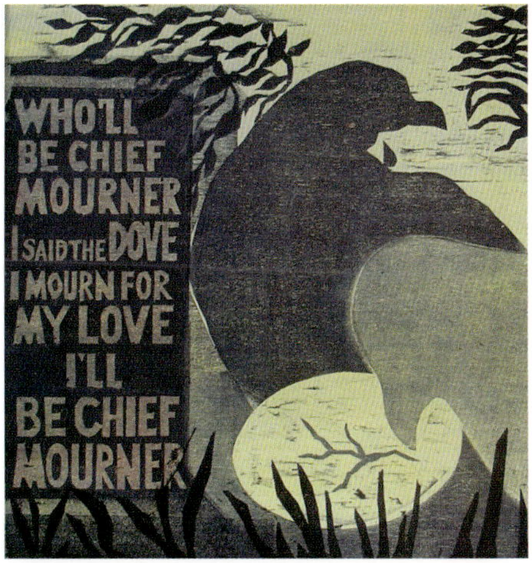

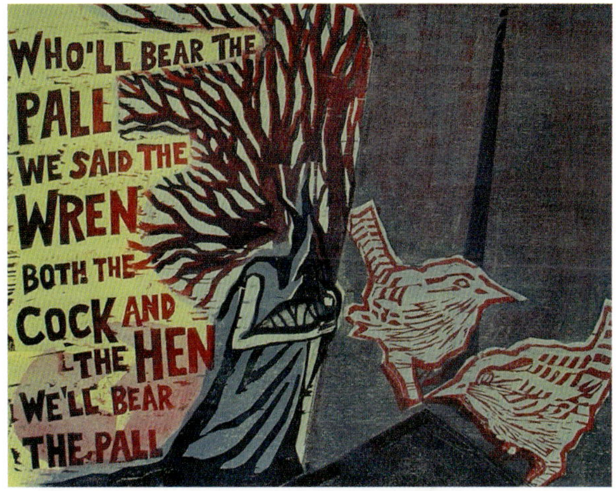

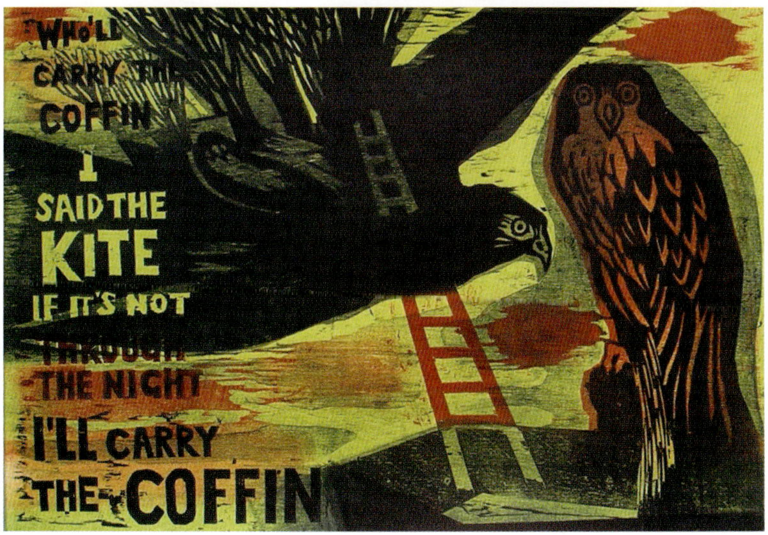

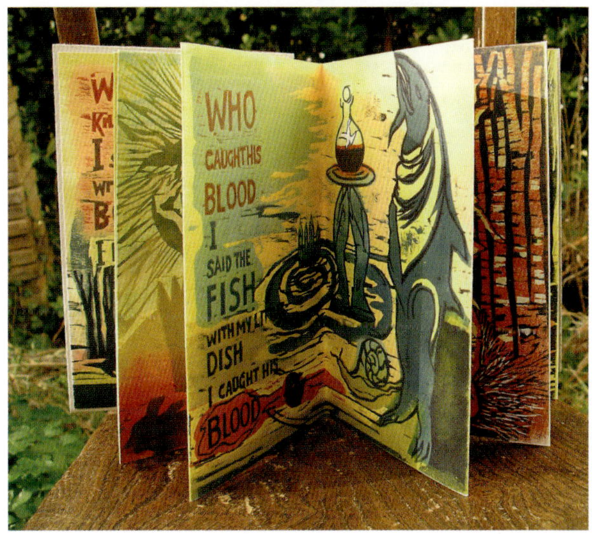

Emma Tuck

www.emmatuck.com
www.flickr.com/photos/emmatuck/

Emma works with paper, ink, paint, pen and pencil. Her compositions are informed by natural forms and patterns – spirals, fissures, branches, waves. It is not however about faithfully representing the natural world; it is about nature as it appears to her – inevitably refracted through the psychological, the political and the trivial. Observing the world relentlessly wounded by human activity she endeavours to capture just a trace of its extraordinary beauty.
She is happy to consider projects or commissions that complement her interests.

1

Common British Insects
12.5 x 18.5 cm
Second-hand book, Rotring pen, pop-ups created from book illustrations

2

Book of Life
9 x 9 [100] cm
Arches paper, Rotring pen, watercolour, collage, rubber stamp, 4 concertina folded books

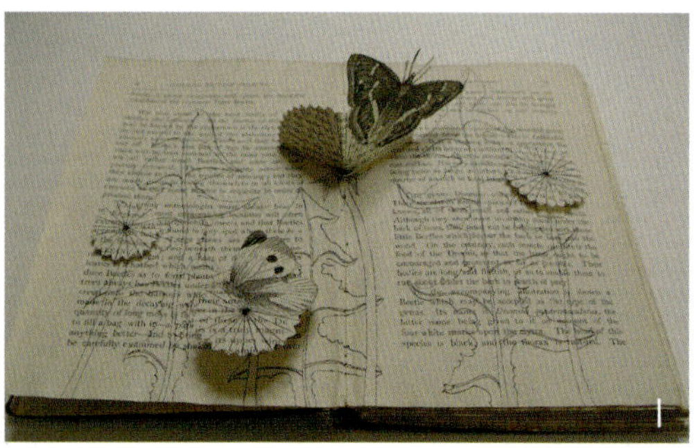

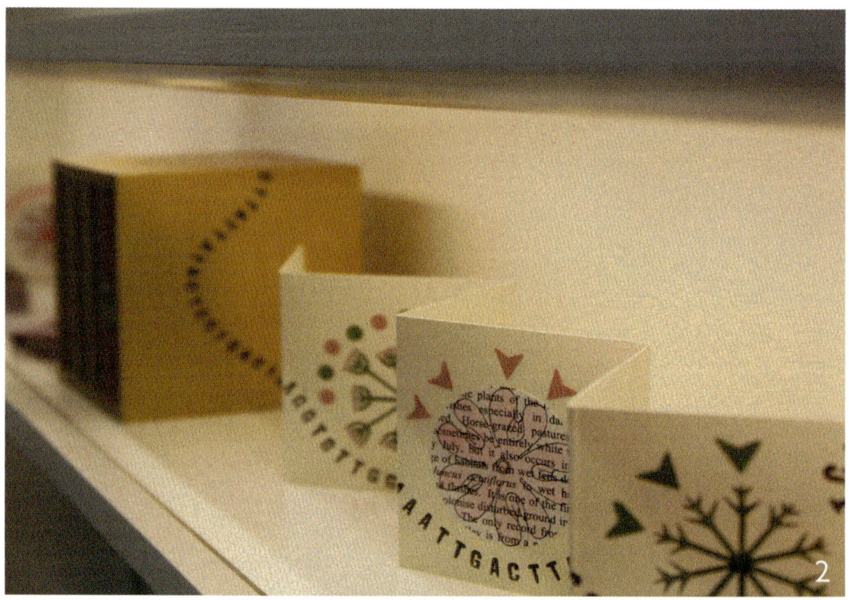

Stephanie Turnbull

tvaussie@aol.com
www.stephanieturnbull.weebly.com

Travelling Suitcase: Barcelona
14 x 11 5. 5 cm Prints, photographs, ephemera, drawings on Japanese paper, handmade objects, fabric, wood and modelling clay

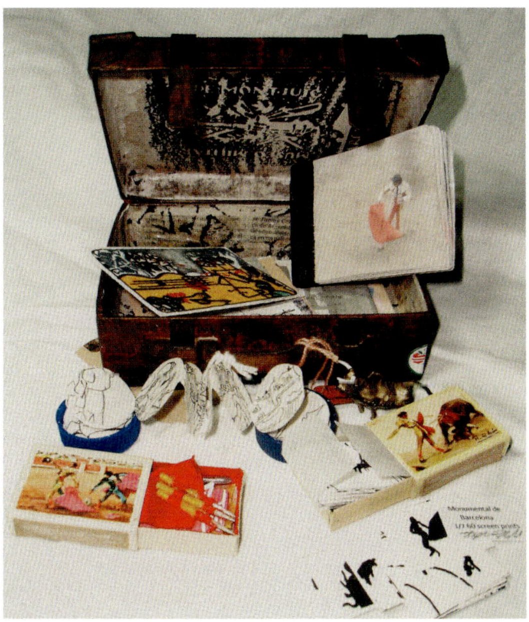

Travelling suitcase: Barcelona is a collection of ephemera, handmade objects, prints, photographs, and drawings. The suitcase documents and traces the artist's time and experience of Barcelona. The outside of the case is covered in apple stickers; rubbings from Parc Guell and Castell de Montjuic line the suitcase; and museum tickets can still be found inside. The used water bottle lids now contain a small book of drawings on Japanese paper. There is a small credit card sized lithographic map of Barcelona, plotting the exact streets and tube stations used during the trip. The suitcase also contains a flip book of video stills taken at a bullfight and two matchboxes. One of these matchboxes houses 60 tiny bullfighting screen prints and the other contains a miniature handmade start-up bullfighting kit, consisting of two capes, a sword, three banderillas and a bull.

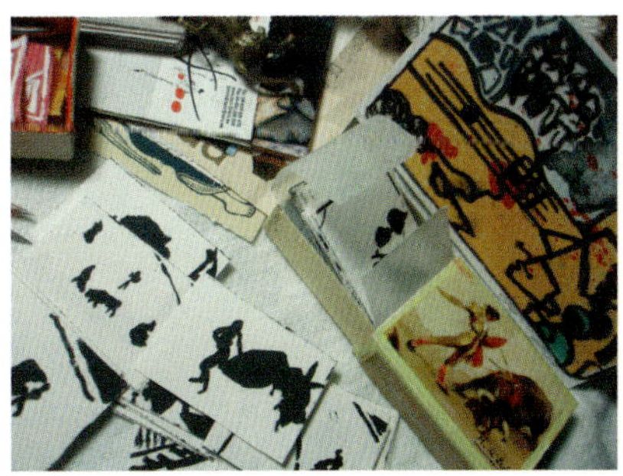

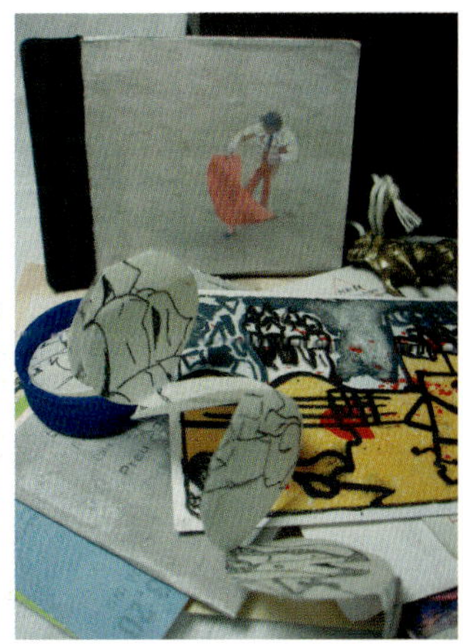

Two Wood Press

andrewmorrisosn@twowoodpress.co.uk
www.twowoodpress.co.uk

Two Wood Press is based in Frith Wood, Chalford, Gloucestershire, where Andrew Morrison and Donald Workman print letterpress from wood and metal type. Images are produced from line blocks, wood and lino-cut as well as through screen-printing. Two Wood Press publishes artists' books, artists' multiples and posters. Besides printing work of their own authorship, they collaborate with book artists and writers, using letterpress sometimes for complete texts, and sometimes for elements within books such as title pages and book jackets.

Printmaking and bookarts are also used in community arts projects. The work produced celebrates the physicality of the hand-made; indent and overlay and the smell of inked pages dried in wood smoke. The range of presses used includes a Colt Armoury platen press, Vicobold platen presses and a Vandercook proofing press.

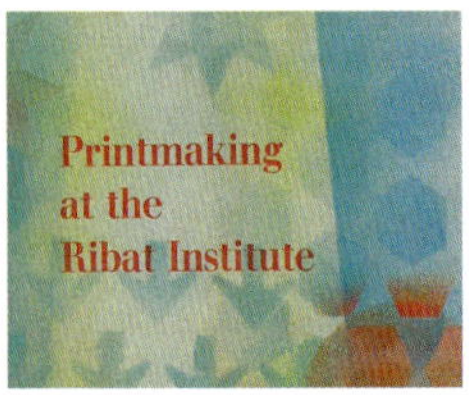

1
Toolbox
55 x 37 cm
Gum arabic & letterpress on Moulin du Gue, Japanese binding

2
Cush Man
58 x 38 cm
Woodcut, letterpress & screenprint on Somerset, Japanese binding

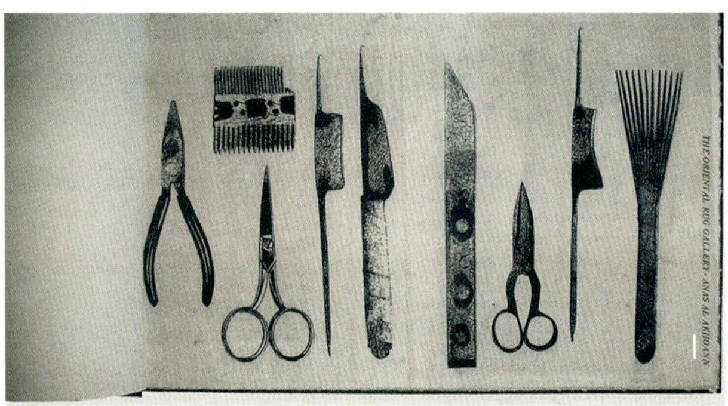

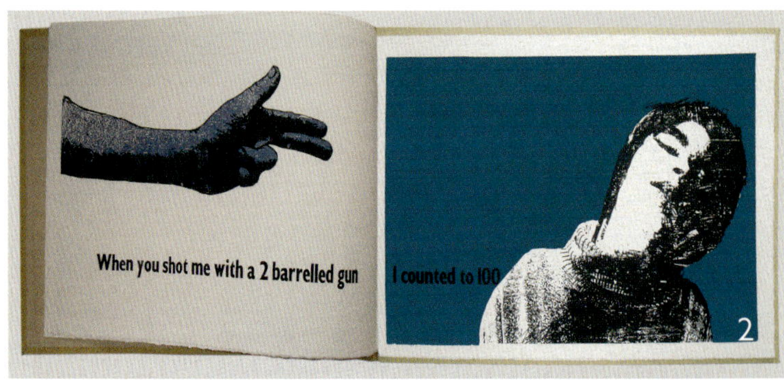

3
Sixties Child
25 x 18 cm
Letterpress & screenprint on Magnani Bookwove, casebound

4
Curlew on Rainslack
15 x 15 cm
Letterpress & screenprint on Somerset, casebound

5
Open West Catalogue
21 x 21 cm
Screenprint & letterpress on Magnani Bookwove, concertina fold

6
Techné
35 x 25 cm
Screenprint & letterpress on Magnani Bookwove, perfect bound

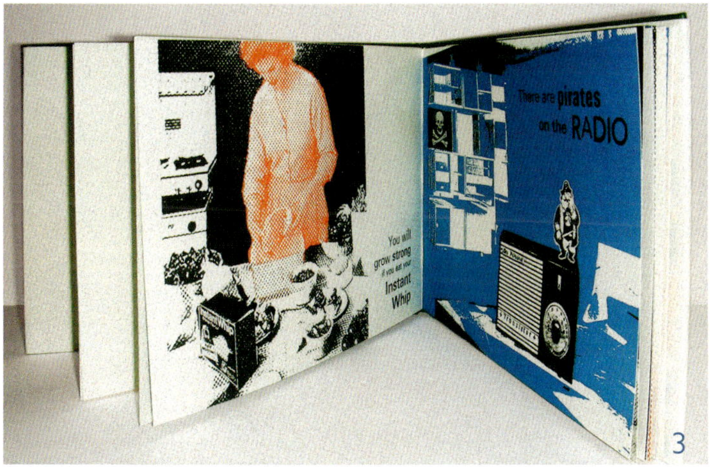

3

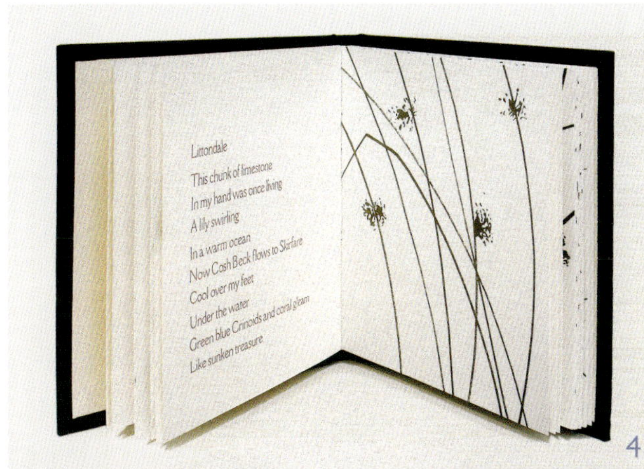

4

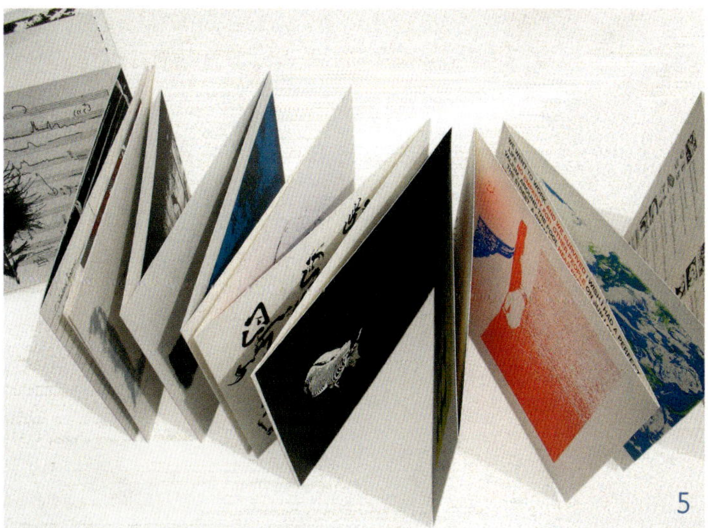
5

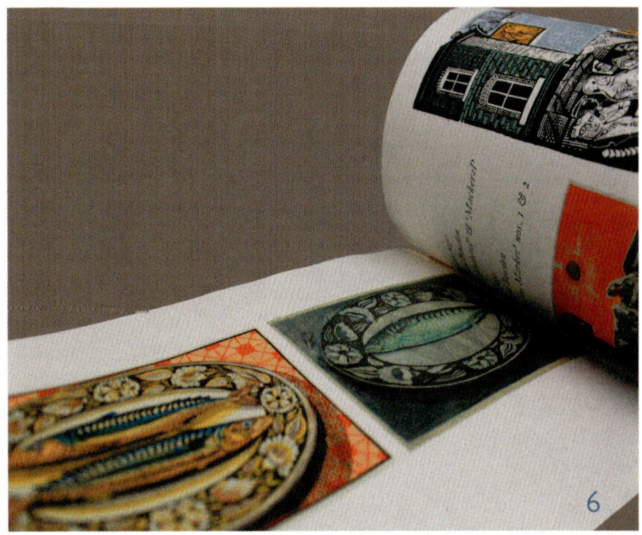
6

Heather Weston
Book Art

heather@bookery.co.uk
www.bookery.co.uk

1
READ (past, tense)
12.5 x 10 cm
Screen-printed with thermochromic ink onto pre-printed paper
Case-bound, 16pp
Open Edition, 2000

2
A Diction
14 x 10 cm
Gmund Bier paper
Angled concertina, 30pp
Open Edition, 2004

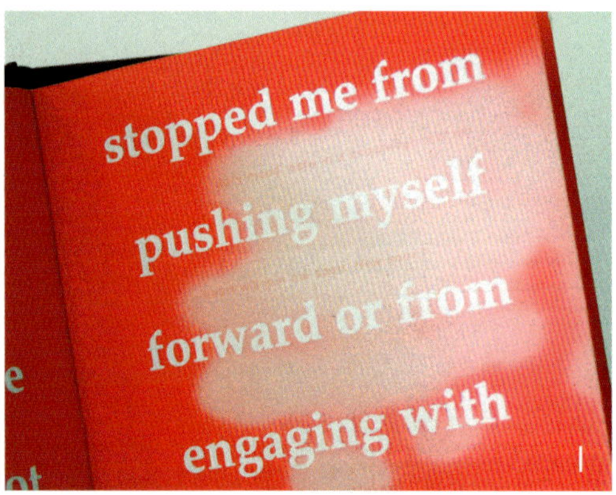

1

Heather Weston's book art explores the psychological and social domain, in book form. She often takes on otherwise taboo or difficult subject matter, allowing the reader a glimpse of the experience contained within, whether it be blushing, alcoholism, self-harm or deafness, amongst others.

Central to the conception and production of all of her books is the intimate marriage of form and content. Here, subject matter, materials, structure and narrative journey are all co-dependent and intertwined, often requiring the reader to actively participate in the completion of the narrative.

Her book art can be viewed in many collections within the UK, including the British Library, National Art Library and the Library at Tate Britain, and across the US in numerous academic and public collections. Heather's books can be purchased, or simply investigated further at: www.bookery.co.uk

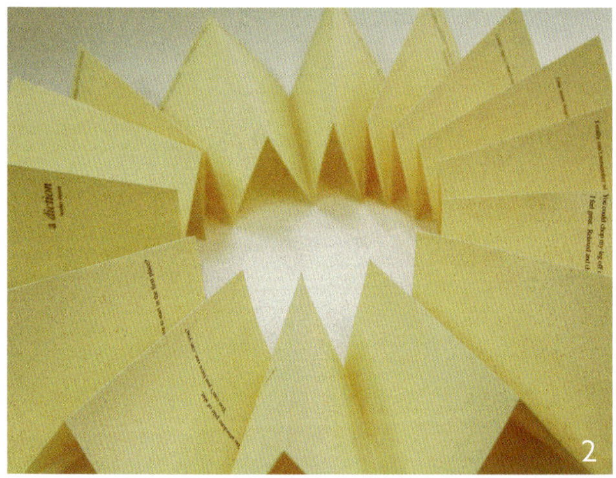
2

3

Flip Read

4 x 9 cm 68pp
Offset Lithography, perfect bound, binding screws. Boxed.
Edition of 150, 2005

4

Paper Cut / relief

13.5 x 7.5 cm
Die-cut and blind embossed, offset lithography. Case-bound concertina, 8pp
Edition of 150, 2007

5

Library of Babel

2m diameter, 7 cm high
Printed acetate, wiro binding
Continuous hexagonal binding. One-off, 2001

6

Borges and I

11 x 11 cm
Black text on black paper, hand embossed
Concertina, 6pp
Open Edition, 2001

7

Borges and I

As HW/04, close-up of hand-embossed text

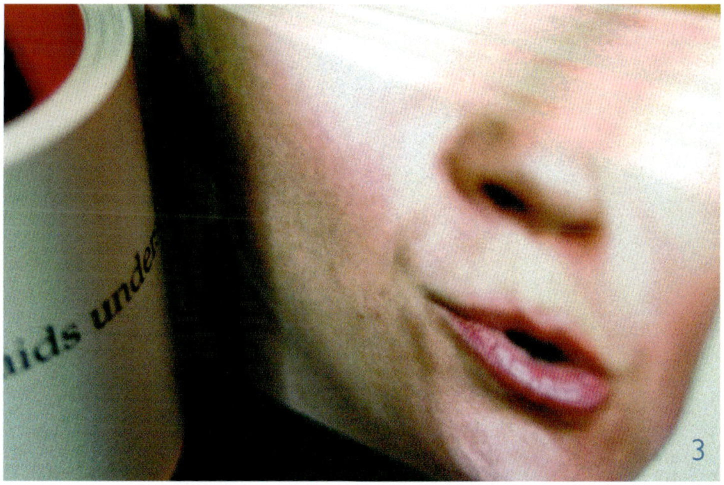

3

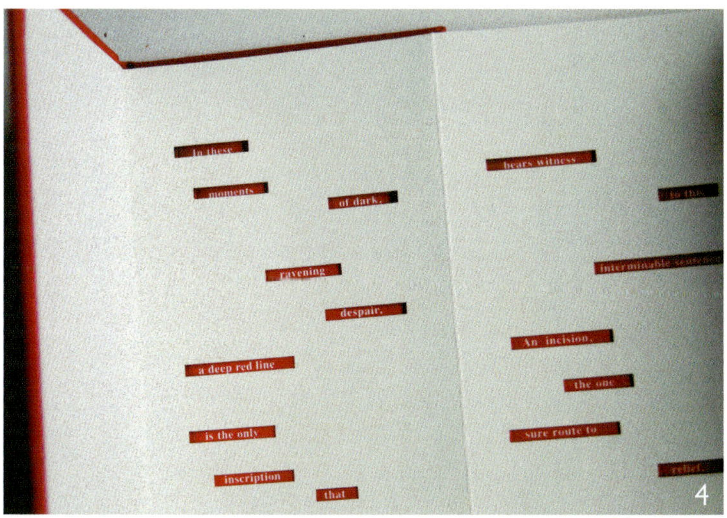

4

5

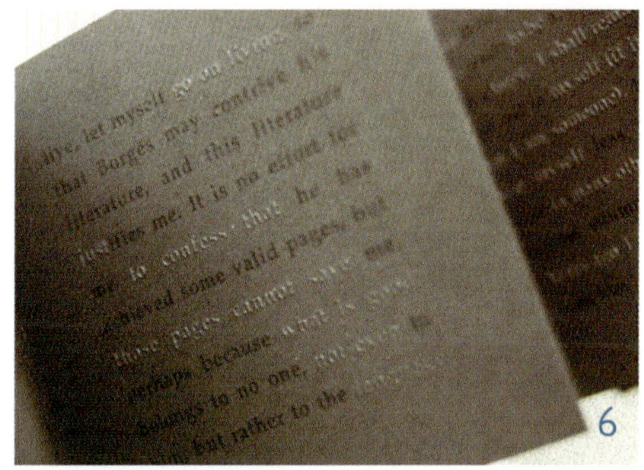

6

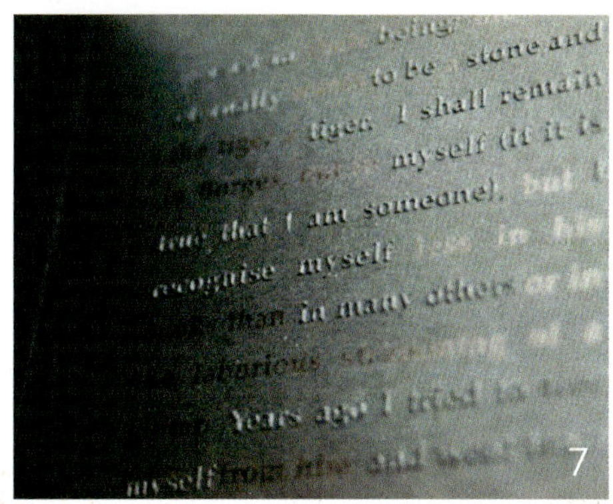

7

Lizanne van Essen

lizanne@vanessen.co.uk
www.vanessen.co.uk

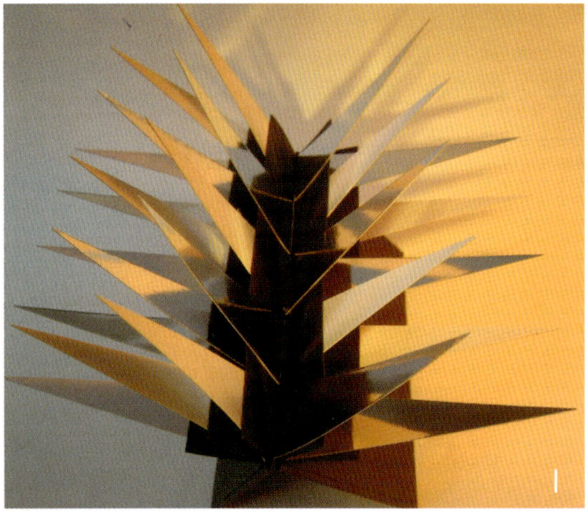

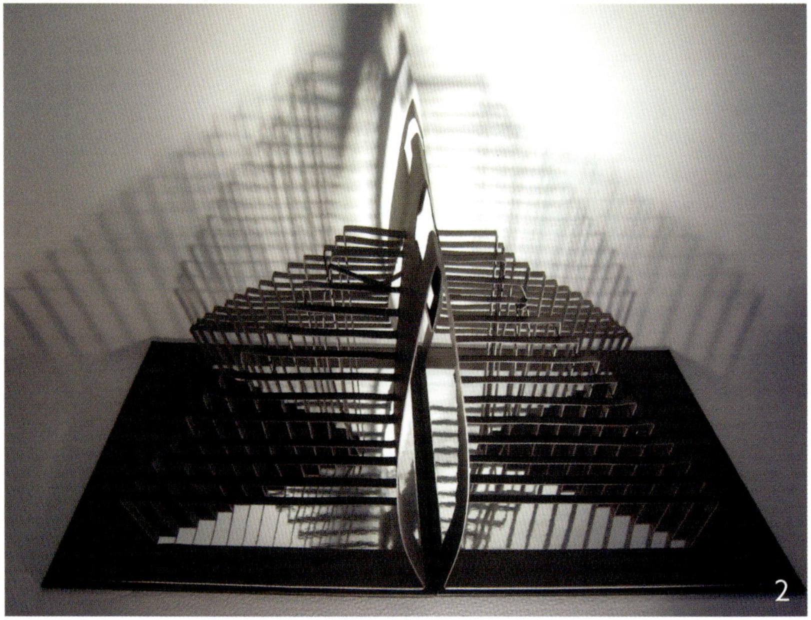

1
Pins and Needles
15.25 x 11 cm closed. Card, hand cut & folded

2
No
18 x 16.5 cm closed. Card, hand cut & folded

3
White Peril
16 x 12 cm closed. Paper & card, hand cut & folded

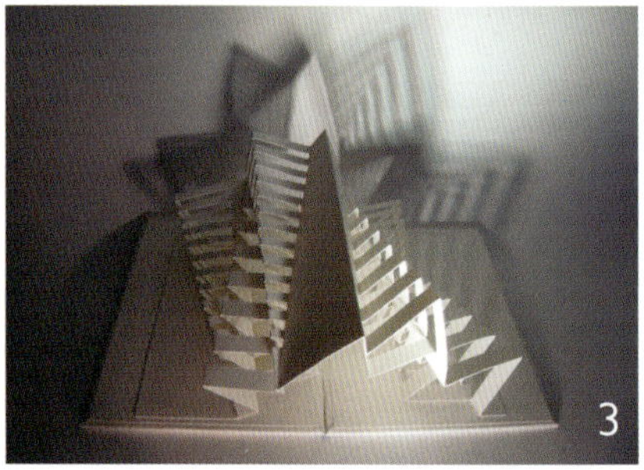

Lynda Wilson

lyndawilson17@hotmail.co.uk
www.lyndawilson.org.uk
www.theartistbookgroup.org.uk

1
Regatta
32 x 26 cm open
Wood, aluminium, Arches paper with screenprint, plastic.

2
Stockbridge Secrets
28 x 28 cm open
Somerset paper and bookcloth with screen - print, greyboard

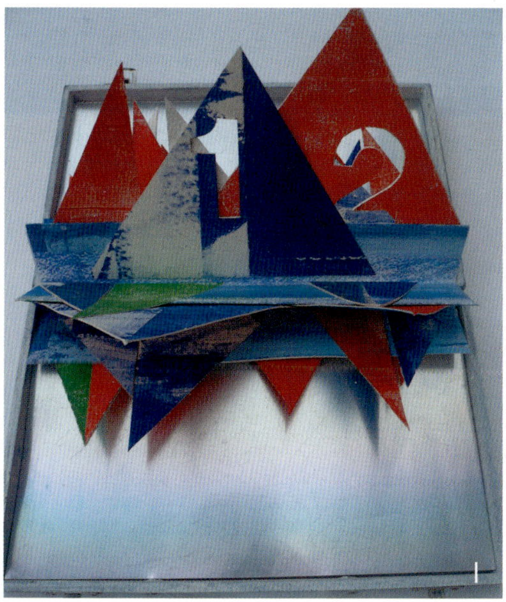

Her passions for the sea and the city – the joy and colour of seaside structures and boats, the layered nature of the city - are all embodied in Lynda's work. The form of the book expresses the contained idea, reinforced by print, pop-up and perforation. As an architect, she loves the three-dimensional opportunities given by artist books, in which capturing the spirit of the place begins from on-site sketching and photography followed by exploration through painting, collage and printmaking in the studio. Lynda lives and works in Edinburgh.

Found objects can develop into books. Regatta started as an old wooden box. The yachts and the sea are held within it; it's a surprise to find what's inside.

Stockbridge Secrets is more muted in tone and conveys the journey through an old part of the city.

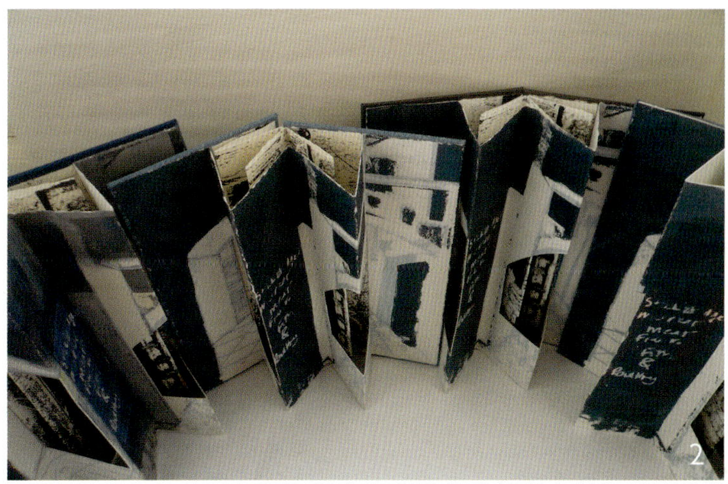

Susie Wilson

susie.wilson2@yahoo.co.uk
www.susiewilson.org
www.theartistbookgroup.org.uk

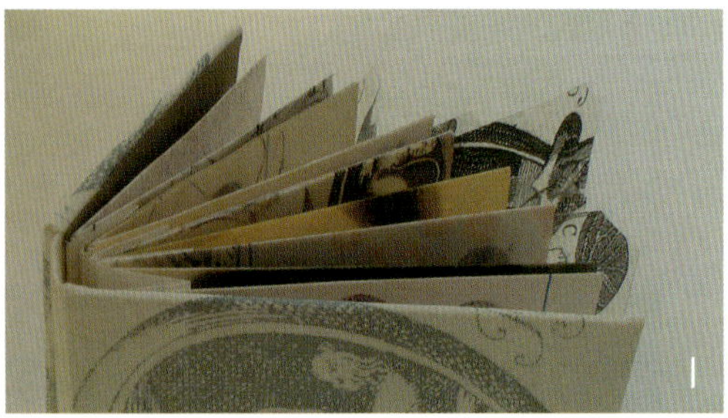

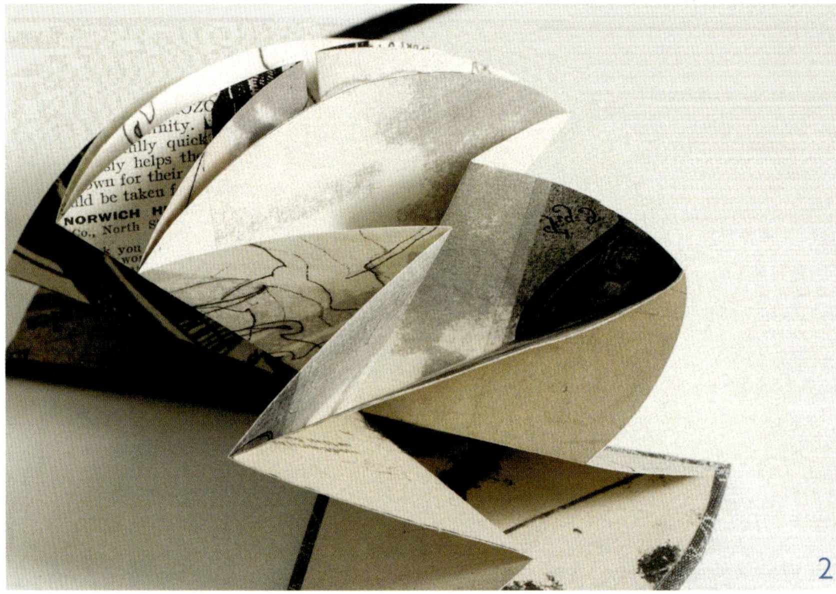

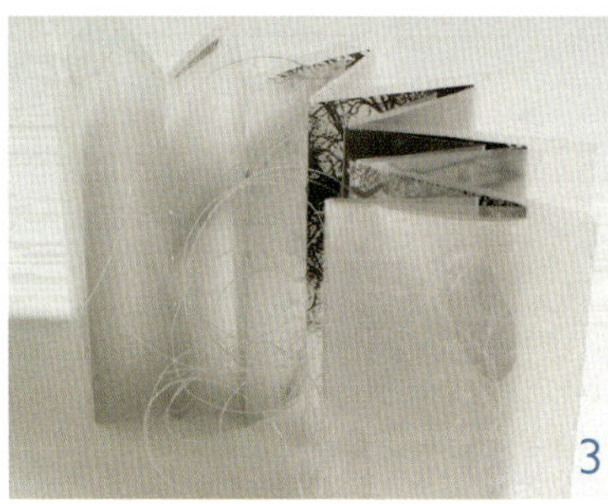

1
Hidden Inside
13 x 7 cm
Screenprint & mixed media with acetates

2
Inside/Outside
8 x 6 cm
Mixed media, digital printing

3
Tangled Up
11 x 6 cm
Screenprint & mixed media. Greyboard, acetate & tracing paper

Ness Woodcock-Dennis

drybumbarefoot@googlemail.com
www.wearestudio3.co.uk
T: 07523965017

1
Boatyard Journal
A4
Wood & copper shipwrights rivets

2
Rapunzel Tower
14 x 4 x 3.5 cm
Illustrated & hand cut pull-out; paper & print

3
A selection of
A4 size journals
Wood, metals & plastics

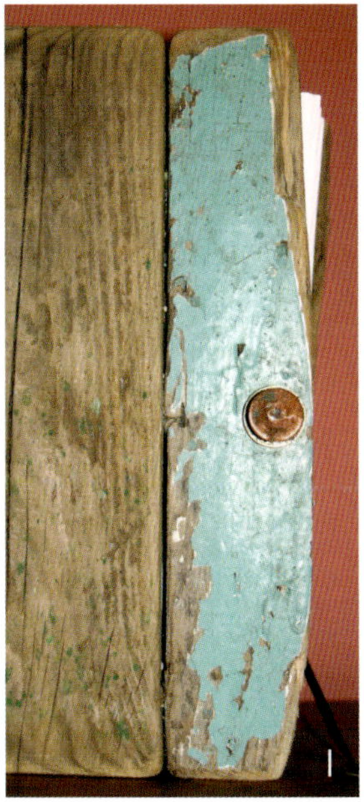

1

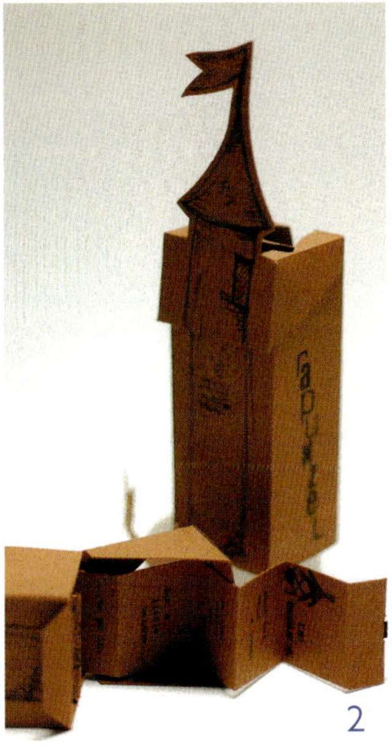

2

Ness Woodcock-Dennis is a painter and journal maker. Her work is inspired by the coastline and the elements using materials sourced from estuary shores, beaches and forests.

The journals are created from found objects including wood, the remains of decaying boats, twisted metals, shreds of tattered flags, and shells to name just a few.

The journals have different levels of meaning and are a creative expression of the fragility of our eco system. This is achieved through the use of discarded materials both natural and man-made. The contrast of the effects of erosion in man-made and natural materials illustrates the power of nature, whilst the concept of a blank journal in itself is simply a creation of a container for 'thoughts and creativity' – a private and safe place of expression.

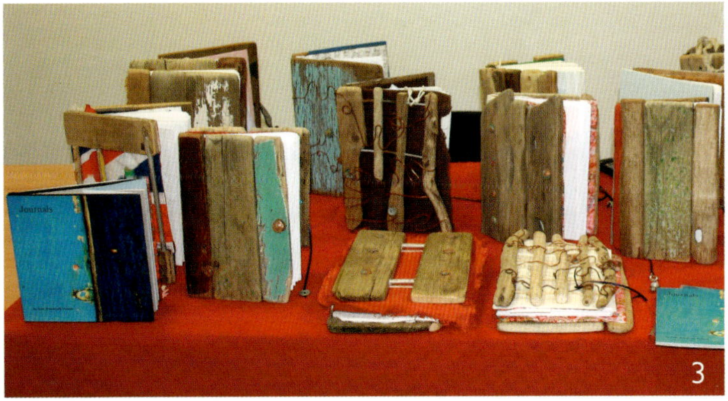

3

The Yellow Fox Press

roscuthbert@hotmail.com
www.theartshed.org.uk

1
'Girls On a Gate'
from 'Bouncing Boy'
24.5 x 33 cm open
Zerkall paper, boxwood block, printing ink

2
Four Small Books
Each 24.5 x 16.5 cms
Card, Zerkall paper,hand stitched,handset text, 3 full page wood engravings

The Yellow Fox Press produces hand made books which celebrate fine poetry illustrated by artist Ros Cuthbert with wood engravings or wood cuts. The editions are numbered and signed by engraver and poet. It has produced four paper covered books and a hard back book:
'Islands' with 3 poems by John Crook and 3 wood engravings
'Birdsong and Water' with 9 poems by Frances Horovitz and 3 engravings
'Nature Studies' with 7 poems by Philip Gross and 4 wood engravings
'Bouncing Boy' with 6 poems by Helen Dunmore and 4 wood engravings
'Hlep!' with 15 poems by Gerard Benson and 4 wood cuts
The books are produced in co-operation with a printer who organises the setting and printing of the text while Ros uses her Columbian press for the engravings.

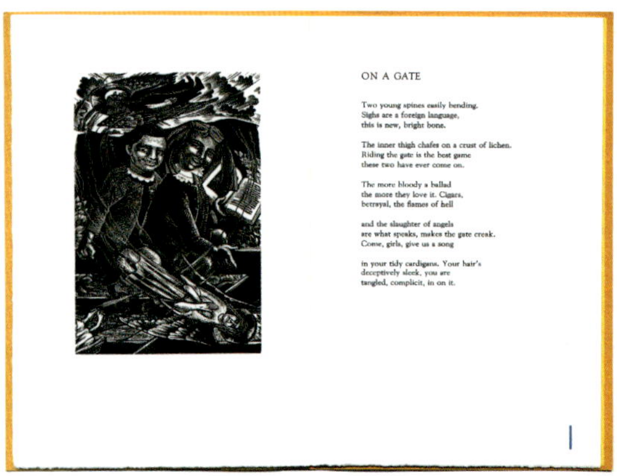

1

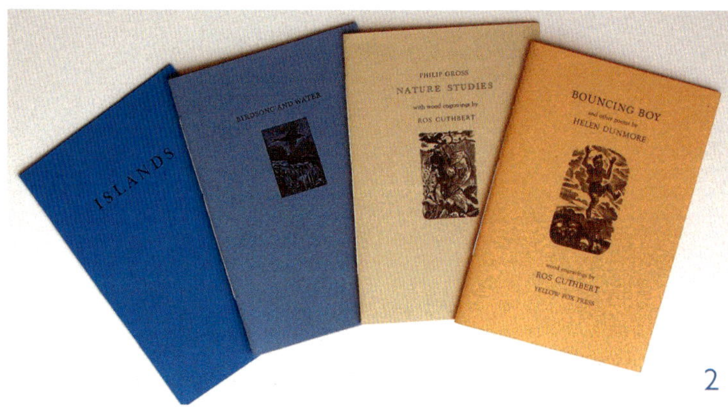

2

3
'R.I.P.' from the special edition of 'Hlep!'
27.5 x 19.8 cm
Zerkall paper, hand set text, woodcut hand tinted in watercolour

4
Hlep! special edition 10 copies with slipcase
27.5 x 19.8 cm
Hand dyed Pentland goat leather, gold line block design on cover, slipcase, woodcuts hand coloured.

5
Hlep! ordinary edition 50 copies
27.3 x 19.8 cm
Zerkall paper, purple buckram, gold blocked design on cover, 4 woodcuts, handset text

6
Dragonflies
15 x 10 cms
Zerkall paper, boxwood block, black printing ink

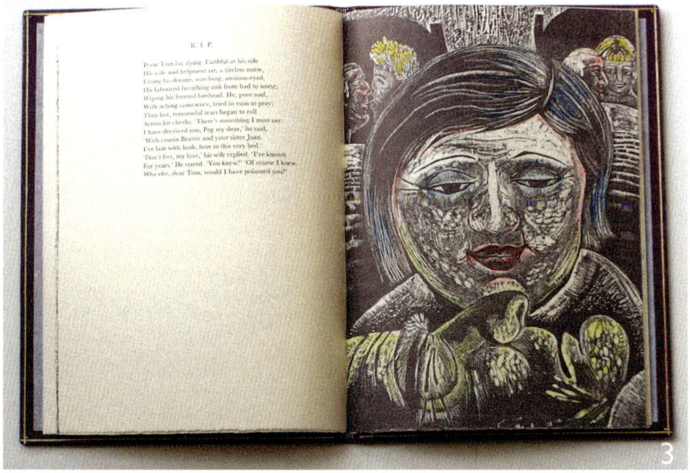

3

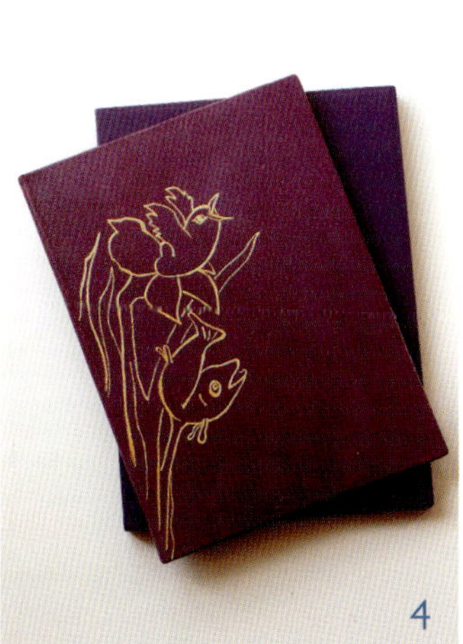

4

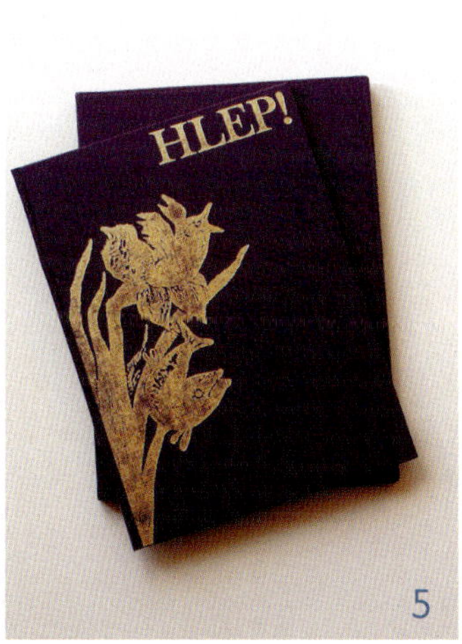

5

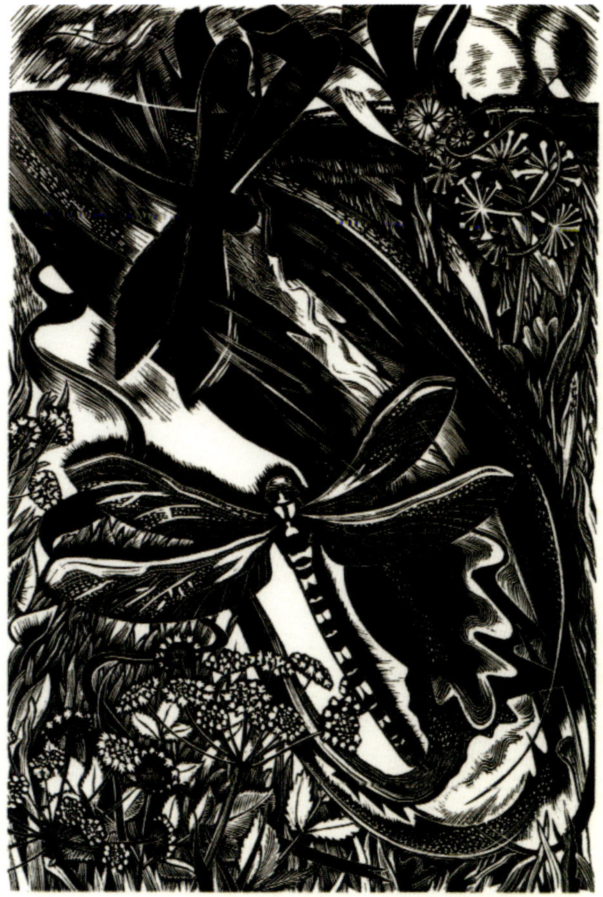

6

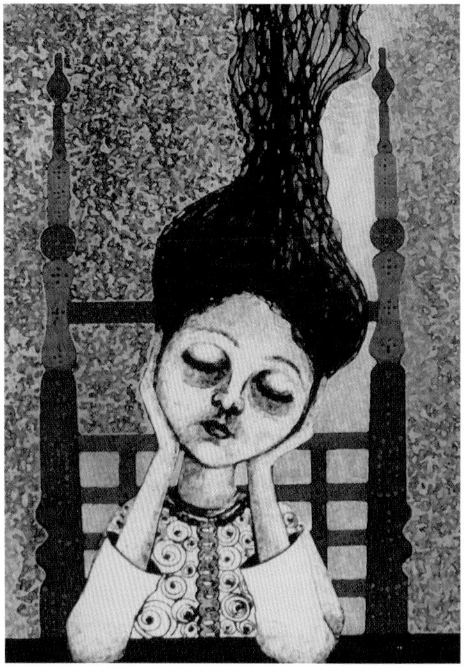

Traveller's Tale by Charlotte Andrew p7

INDEX

Index